Marriage,
Family,
& Sexuality

Marriage, Family, & Sexuality

PROBING THE HEADLINES THAT IMPACT YOUR FAMILY

Kerby Anderson

General Editor

kregel
PUBLICATIONS

Grand Rapids, MI 49501

Marriage, Family, & Sexuality: Probing the Headlines That Impact Your Family

Published by Kregel Publications, a division of Kregel, Inc., P.O. Box 2607, Grand Rapids, MI 49501. Kregel Publications provides trusted, biblical publications for Christian growth and service. Your comments and suggestions are valued.

Unless otherwise indicated, Scripture taken from the *Holy Bible: New International Version*®. © 1973, 1978, 1984 by International Bible Society. Used by permission of Zondervan Publishing House. All rights reserved.

Scripture quotations marked NASB are from the *New American Standard Bible,* © the Lockman Foundation 1960, 1962, 1963, 1968, 1971, 1972, 1973, 1975, 1977.

Scripture quotations marked KJV are from the King James Version.

For more information about Kregel Publications, visit our web site: www.kregel.com

Library of Congress Cataloging-in-Publication Data
Anderson, J. Kerby.
  Marriage, family, & sexuality: probing the headlines that impact your famliy / edited by Kerby Anderson.
       p.   cm.—
Includes bibliographical references.
    1. Sex—Religious aspects—Christianity.
2. Marriage—Religious aspects—Christianity.
3. Christian ethics.   I. Title.
BT708.A5   1999   261.8'357—dc 21   99-33450
                                                           CIP

ISBN 0-8254-2031-8

Printed in the United States of America

1 2 3 4 5 / 04 03 02 01 00

Contents

Foreword

I can still recall my mom giving me a briar patch "mission" when I was a boy. When she had sprayed me sufficiently with mosquito and tick repellent, she would equip me with a bucket and send me out to pick blackberries. I can still recall the sweet, flavorful nectar of a mouthful of fresh, ripe berries, the heat of the July sun, and the thorns.

Ah yes, the thorns.

To a small boy the briar patch looked like a forbidding mountain of thorns. It always seemed that the mother lode of blackberries was just beyond easy reach. My most careful efforts to safely mine the fruit inevitably resulted in my legs, arms, and chest getting pricked and scratched by a million thorns. It took courage to "attack" that thorny thicket because it was also home to poison ivy, ticks, chiggers, and even snakes.

I've always admired people who are willing to go into a briar patch—as are Kerby Anderson and his associates at Probe Ministries. They've never let a good "briar patch" keep them from aggressively tackling the issues of the day. And that's what *Marriage, Family, & Sexuality* is all about: courageous men and women intelligently and persuasively challenging the "thorny" places that cause most of us to stand at a distance.

This book is a briar patch of cultural issues with Christian responses. Kerby and some good friends at Probe have trudged headlong into issues like divorce, homosexuality, sexually transmitted diseases, premarital sex, and more. In doing so, they have carved a path through these prickly places in an effort to give you the confidence, understanding, and courage you need to stand up for what is right.

These gifted apologists answer the challenges of our culture by calling individual Christians to draw biblical lines and develop Christian convictions. *Marriage, Family, & Sexuality* will equip you with the biblical tools you need to stand strong in a culture that punishes those who hold Christian beliefs. This book ought to be packed in the suitcase of all graduating seniors as they leave home and head for college, work, or service.

I recommend this work to you. And I encourage you to jump into a few briar patches of you own.

DENNIS RAINEY
EXECUTIVE DIRECTOR, FAMILYLIFE

Contributors

Kerby Anderson is the president of Probe Ministries International. He received a B.S. from Oregon State University, an M.F.S. from Yale University, and an M.S. from Georgetown University. He is the author of several books, including *Genetic Engineering, Origin Science, Living Ethically in the 90s, Signs of Warning—Signs of Hope,* and *Moral Dilemmas.* He is a nationally syndicated columnist whose editorials have appeared in the *Dallas Morning News,* the *Miami Herald,* the *San Jose Mercury,* and the *Houston Post.* He is the host of the *Probe* radio program and frequently serves as guest host on *Point of View* (USA Radio Network) and *Open Line* (Moody Broadcasting Network).

Ray Bohlin is the executive director of Probe Ministries. He is a graduate of the University of Illinois (B.S., zoology), North Texas State University (M.S., population genetics), and the University of Texas at Dallas (M.S., Ph.D., molecular biology). He is a co-author of the book *Natural Limits to Biological Change* and has published numerous journal articles. He was named a 1997–98 Research Fellow of the Discovery Institute's Center for the Renewal of Science and Culture.

Sue Bohlin is an associate speaker with Probe. She attended the University of Illinois and Trinity Evangelical Divinity School and has been a Bible teacher and Christian speaker for more than twenty years. In addition to being a professional calligrapher, she also manages Probe's web site.

Rick Rood is the former director of publications at Probe Ministries and now serves as a hospital chaplain. He is a graduate of Seattle Pacific University (B.A., history) and Dallas Theological Seminary (Th.M.). He has pursued Ph.D. studies in theology at DTS and has served as a pastor, been a seminary instructor, and worked for a number of years in ministry to international students.

Jerry Solomon is the field director and *Mind Games* co-ordinator of Probe Ministries. He received a B.A. (summa cum laude) in Bible and an M.A. (cum laude) in history and theology from Criswell College. He also has attended the University of North Texas, Canal Zone College, and Lebanon Valley College. In the past, Jerry has worked as a youth pastor. He is the author of *Sheep Among Wolves.*

Jimmy Williams is the founder and former president of Probe Ministries. He is currently minister-at-large. Jimmy has been involved in ministry to young adults and Christians of all ages for forty years. He graduated with a B.A. from Southern Methodist University and a Th.M. from Dallas Theological Seminary. He has pursued inter-disciplinary doctoral studies (A.B.D.) in humanities at the University of Texas at Dallas. He was involved in the Campus Crusade for Christ ministry from 1961 to 1973.

Part 1
Sexual Issues

1

Teen Sexual Revolution

Kerby Anderson

One of the low points in television history occurred September 25, 1991. The program was *Doogie Howser, M.D.* This half-hour TV show, aimed at preteen and teenage kids, focused on the trials and tribulations of an eighteen-year-old child prodigy who graduated from medical school and was in the midst of medical practice. Most programs dealt with the problems of being a kid in an adult's profession. But on September 25, the "problem" Doogie Howser confronted was the fact that he was still a virgin.

Advance publicity drove the audience numbers to unanticipated levels. Millions of parents, teenagers, and pajamas-clad kids sat down in front of their televisions to watch Doogie Howser and his girlfriend Wanda deal with his "problem." Twenty minutes into the program, they completed the act. Television ratings went through the roof. Parents and advertisers should have as well.

What is wrong with this picture? Each day approximately seventy-seven hundred teenagers relinquish their virginity. In the process, many will become pregnant and many more will contract a sexually transmitted disease (STD). Already one in four Americans have an STD, and this percentage is increasing each year. Weren't the producers of *Doogie Howser, M.D.* aware that teenage pregnancy and STDs are exploding in the population? Didn't they stop and think of the consequences of portraying virginity as a "problem" to be rectified? Why weren't parents and advertisers concerned about the message this program was sending?

Perhaps the answer is the trite, age-old refrain "everybody's doing it." Every television network and nearly every TV program deals with sensuality. Sooner or later the values of every other program were bound to show up on a TV program aimed at preteens and teenagers. In many ways the media is merely reflecting a culture that was transformed by a sexual revolution of values. Sexually liberal elites have hijacked our culture by seizing control of two major arenas. The first is the entertainment media (television, movies, rock music, MTV). The second is education (sex education classes and school-based clinics). These two forces have transformed the social landscape of America and made promiscuity a virtue and virginity a "problem" to be solved.

The Teenage Sexuality Crisis

We face a teenage sexuality crisis in America. Consider these alarming statistics of children having children. A *New York Times* article reported: "Some studies indicate three-fourths of all girls have had sex during their teenage years and 15 percent have had four or more partners."[1] A Lou Harris poll commissioned by Planned Parenthood discovered that 46 percent of sixteen-year-olds and 57 percent of seventeen-year-olds have had sexual intercourse.[2]

Former Secretary of Education William Bennett in speaking to the National School Board Association warned, "The statistics by which we measure how our children—

how our boys and girls—are treating one another sexually are little short of staggering." He found that more than one-half of America's young people have had sexual intercourse by the time they are seventeen. He also found that more than one million teenage girls in the United States become pregnant each year. Of those who give birth, nearly half are not yet eighteen.

"These numbers," William Bennett concluded, "are an irrefutable indictment of sex education's effectiveness in reducing teenage sexual activity and pregnancies." Moreover, these numbers are not skewed by impoverished, inner city youths from broken homes. One New York polling firm posed questions to thirteen hundred students in sixteen suburban high schools in areas to get a reading of "mainstream" adolescent attitudes. They discovered that 57 percent lost virginity in high school, and 79 percent lost virginity by the end of college. The average age for sex was 16.9. Thirty-three percent of high school students had sex once a month to once a week, and 52 percent of college students had sex once a month to once a week.[3]

Kids are trying sex at an earlier age than ever before. More than a third of fifteen-year-old boys have had sexual intercourse as have 27 percent of fifteen-year-old girls. Among sexually active teenage girls, 61 percent have had multiple partners. The reasons for such early sexual experimentation are many:

- *Biology.* Teenagers are maturing faster sexually due to better health and nutrition. Since the turn of the century, for example, the onset of menstruation in girls has occurred three months younger each decade. Consequently, urges that used to arise in the mid-teens now explode in the early teens. Meanwhile, the typical age of first marriages has risen more than four years since the 1950s.

- *A sex-saturated society.* Sex is used to sell everything from cars to toothpaste. Sexual innuendoes clutter most every TV program and movie. And explicit nudity and sensuality that used to be reserved for R-rated movies have found their way into the home through broadcast and cable television. Media researchers calculate that teenagers see approximately five hours of TV a day. This means that they see each year nearly fourteen thousand sexual encounters on television alone.

- *Lack of parental supervision and direction.* Working parents and reductions in after-school programs have left teenagers with less supervision and a looser after-school life. In the inner city, the scarcity of jobs and parents coupled with a cynical view of the future invites teenage promiscuity and its inevitable consequences. Adolescent boys in the suburbs trying to prove their masculinity form groups like the infamous score-keeping Spur Posse gang in California.

Even when teenagers want to sit out the sexual revolution, they often get little help from parents who may be too embarrassed or intimidated to talk to their children. Parents, in fact, often lag behind their kids in sexual information. At one sex education workshop held by Girls Inc. (formerly Girls Club of America), nearly half of the mothers had never seen a condom. Other mothers did not want to discuss sex because they were molested as children and were fearful of talking about sex with their daughters.

Teenagers are also getting mixed messages. In any given week, they are likely to hear contradictory messages: "No sex until you're married." "No sex unless you're older." "No sex unless you're protected." "No sex unless you're in love." No wonder adolescents are confused.

The Report Card on Sex Education

For more than thirty years proponents of comprehensive sex education have told us that giving sexual information to young children and adolescents will reduce the number of unplanned pregnancies and sexually transmitted diseases. In that effort, nearly $3 billion has been spent on federal Title X family planning services, yet teenage pregnancies and abortions rise.

Perhaps one of the most devastating popular critiques of comprehensive sex education came from Barbara Dafoe Whitehead. The journalist who said that Dan Quayle was right also was willing to say that sex education was wrong. Her *Atlantic Monthly* article entitled "The Failure of Sex Education," demonstrated that sex education neither reduced pregnancy nor slowed the spread of STDs.[4]

Comprehensive sex education is mandated in at least seventeen states, so Whitehead chose one state and focused her analysis on the sex education experiment in New Jersey. Like other curricula, New Jersey's *Learning About Family Life* sex education program rests on certain questionable assumptions:

1. Children are sexual from birth. Sex educators reject the classic notion of a latency period until approximately age twelve. They argue that you are "being sexual when you throw your arms around your grandpa and give him a hug."

2. Children are sexually miseducated. Parents, in their view, have simply not done their job, so we need

"professionals" to do it right. Parents try to protect their children, fail to affirm their sexuality, and even discuss sexuality in a context of moralizing. The media, they say, is also guilty of providing sexual misinformation.

3. If miseducation is the problem, then sex education in the schools is the solution. Parents are failing miserably at the task, so "it is time to turn the job over to the schools. Schools occupy a safe middle ground between Mom and MTV."[5]

While *Learning About Family Life* discusses such things as sexual desire, AIDS, divorce, condoms, and masturbation, it nearly ignores such issues as abstinence, marriage, self-control, and virginity. One technique promoted to prevent pregnancy and STDs is noncoital sex, or what some sex educators call outercourse. Yet there is good evidence to suggest that teaching teenagers to explore their sexuality through noncoital techniques will lead to coitus. Ultimately, outercourse will lead to intercourse.

Whitehead concludes that comprehensive sex education has been a failure. For example, the percent of teenage births to unwed mothers was 67 percent in 1980 and rose to 84 percent in 1991. In the place of this failed curriculum, Whitehead describes a better program. She found that "sex education works best when it combines clear messages about behavior with strong moral and logistical support for the behavior sought."[6] One example she cites is the Postponing Sexual Involvement program at Grady Memorial Hospital in Atlanta, Georgia, which offers more than a "Just Say No" message. It reinforces the message by having adolescents practice the desired behavior and enlists the aid of older teenagers to teach younger teenagers how to resist sexual advances. Whitehead also found that "religiously observant teens" are less likely to experiment sexually, thus providing an opportunity for church-related programs to stem the tide of teenage pregnancy. The results of Whitehead's research are clear: abstinence is still the best form of sex education.

Is "Safe Sex" Really Safe?

At the 1987 World Congress of Sexologists, Theresa Crenshaw asked the audience, "If you had the available partner of your dreams and knew that person carried HIV, how many of you would have sex, depending on a condom for your protection?" When they were asked for a show of hands, none of the eight-hundred-member audience indicated that they would trust the condoms.[7] If condoms do not eliminate the fear of HIV infection for sexologists and sex educators, why do we encourage the children of America to play STD Russian roulette?

Are condoms a safe and effective way to reduce pregnancy and STDs? To listen to sex educators you would think so. Every day sex education classes throughout this country promote condoms as a means of safe sex or at least safer sex. But the research on condoms provides no such guarantee.

For example, Texas researcher Susan Weller, writing in the 1993 issue of *Social Science Medicine,* evaluated all research published prior to July 1990 on condom effectiveness. She reported that condoms are only 87 percent effective in preventing pregnancy and 69 percent effective in reducing the risk of HIV infection.[8] This translates into a 31 percent failure rate in preventing AIDS transmission. And according to a study in the 1992 *Family Planning Perspectives,* 15 percent of married couples who use condoms for birth control end up with an unplanned pregnancy within the first year.[9]

So why has condom distribution become the center-piece of the United States AIDS policy and the most frequently promoted aspect of comprehensive sex education? For many years, the answer to that question was an *a priori* commitment to condoms and a safe sex message over an abstinence message. But in recent years, sex educators and public health officials have been pointing to one study which appeared to vindicate the condom policy.

The study was presented at the Ninth International Conference on AIDS held in Berlin on June 9, 1993. The study involved 304 couples with one partner who was HIV positive. Of the 123 couples who used condoms with each act of sexual intercourse, not a single negative HIV partner became positive.[10] So proponents of condom distribution thought they had scientific vindication for their views.

Unfortunately that is not the whole story. Condoms do appear to be effective in stopping the spread of AIDS when used "correctly and consistently." Most individuals, however, do not use them "correctly and consistently." What happens to them? Well, it turns out that part of the study received much less attention. Of 122 couples who could not be taught to use condoms properly, twelve became HIV positive in both partners. Undoubtedly over time, even more partners would contract AIDS.

How well does this study apply to the general population? I would argue the couples in the study group were quite dissimilar from the general population. For example, they knew the HIV status of their spouse and therefore had a vested interest in protecting themselves. They were responsible partners and in a committed monogamous relationship. In essence, their actions and attitudes differ dramatically from teenagers and single adults who do not know the HIV status of their partners, are often reckless, and have multiple sexual partners.

Contrary to popular belief, condoms are not as reliable as public health pronouncements might lead you to think. Abstinence is still the only safe sex.

Only Abstinence Programs Work

Less than a decade ago, an abstinence-only program was rare in the public schools. Today, directive abstinence programs can be found in many school districts while battles are fought in other school districts for their inclusion or removal. While proponents of abstinence programs run for school boards or influence existing school board members, groups like Planned Parenthood bring lawsuits against districts that use abstinence-based curricula, arguing that they are inaccurate or incomplete. At least a dozen abstinence-based curricula are on the market, with the largest being *Sex Respect* (Bradley, Illinois) and *Teen-Aid* (Spokane, Washington).

The emergence of abstinence-only programs as an alternative to comprehensive sex education programs was due to both popularity and politics. Parents concerned about the ineffectiveness of the safe-sex message eagerly embraced the message of abstinence. And political funding helped spread the message and legitimize its educational value. The Adolescent Family Life Act enacted in 1981 by the Reagan Administration created Title XX and set aside 2 million dollars a year for the development and implementation of abstinence-based programs. Although the Clinton Administration later cut funding for abstinence programs, the earlier funding in the 1980s helped groups like Sex Respect and Teen-Aid launch abstinence programs in the schools.

Parents and children have embraced the abstinence message in significant numbers. One national poll by the

University of Chicago found that 68 percent of adults surveyed said premarital sex among teenagers is "always wrong." A 1994 poll for *USA Weekend* asked more than twelve hundred teens and adults what they thought of "several high profile athletes [who] are saying in public that they have abstained from sex before marriage and are telling teens to do the same." Seventy-two percent of the teens and 78 percent of the adults said they agree with the pro-abstinence message.[11]

Promoting Abstinence Pays

Their enthusiasm for abstinence-only education is well founded. Even though the abstinence message has been criticized by some as naive or inadequate, there are good reasons to promote abstinence in schools and society.

1. Teenagers want to learn about abstinence. Contrary to the often repeated teenage claim, not "everyone's doing it." A 1992 study by the Center for Disease Control found that 43 percent of teenagers (ages fourteen to seventeen) had engaged in sexual intercourse at least once.[12] Put another way, the latest surveys suggest that a majority of teenagers are *not* doing it.
2. Abstinence prevents pregnancy. Proponents of abstinence-only programs argue that it will significantly lower the teenage pregnancy rate and cite lots of anecdotes and statistics to make their case. For example, the San Marcos Junior High in San Marcos, California, adopted an abstinence-only program developed by Teen-Aid. The curriculum dropped the school's pregnancy rate from 147 to twenty within a two-year period.[13] An abstinence-only program for girls in Washington, D.C., has seen only one of four hundred girls become pregnant.[14]

3. Abstinence prevents sexually transmitted diseases (STDs). After more than three decades, the sexual revolution has taken lots of prisoners. Before 1960 there were only two STDs that doctors were concerned about: syphilis and gonorrhea. Today, there are more than twenty significant STDs, ranging from the relatively harmless to the fatal. Twelve million Americans are newly infected each year, and 63 percent of these new infections are in people less than twenty-five years old. Eighty percent of those infected with an STD have absolutely no symptoms.

The conclusion is simple: Abstinence is the only truly safe sex.

2

Sexually Transmitted Diseases

Ray Bohlin

S exually transmitted diseases (or STDs) are spreading to unprecedented and epidemic proportions. Thirty years of the sexual revolution is paying an ugly dividend. While a few STDs can be transmitted apart from sex acts, all are transmissible by the exchange of bodily fluids during intimate sexual contact. I want to discuss the severity of the problem as well as what must be done to save a majority of the next generation from the shame, infertility, and sometimes death that can result from STDs.

The information I am about to share is from data gathered by the Medical Institute for Sexual Health of Austin, Texas.[1] All of these statistics are readily available from reputable medical and scientific journals.

Today, there are approximately twenty-five STDs. A few can be fatal. Many women are living in fear of what their future may hold as a result of STD infection. It is estimated that one in five Americans between the ages of fifteen and fifty-five are currently infected with one or more STDs, and 12 million Americans are newly infected each year. That's nearly 5 percent of the entire population of the United States. Of these new infections, 63 percent are in people less than twenty-five years old.

This epidemic is a recent phenomenon. Some young people have parents who may have had multiple sexual partners with relative impunity. They may conclude that they too are safe from disease. However, most of these diseases were not around twenty to thirty years ago. Prior to 1960, there were only two significant sexually transmitted diseases: syphilis and gonorrhea. Both were easily treated with antibiotics. In the sixties and seventies this relatively stable situation began to change. For example, in 1976, chlamydia first appeared in increasing numbers in the United States. Chlamydia, particularly dangerous to women, is now the most common STD in the country.

Then in 1981, human immunodeficiency virus (HIV), the virus which causes AIDS, was identified. By early 1993, between 1 and 2 million Americans were infected with AIDS, over 12 million were infected worldwide, and over 160 thousand had died in the United States alone. Over 10 percent of the total U.S. population, 30 million people, are infected with herpes.

In 1985, human papilloma virus (HPV), began to increase. This virus results in venereal warts and will often lead to deadly cancers.

In 1990, penicillin resistant strains of gonorrhea were present in all fifty states.

By 1992, syphilis was at a forty-year high. As of 1993, pelvic inflammatory disease (PID), which is almost always caused by gonorrhea or chlamydia, was affecting 1 million new women each year. This includes sixteen to twenty thousand teenagers. This complication causes pelvic pain and infertility and is the leading cause of hospitalization for women, apart from pregnancy, during the childbearing years.

Pelvic inflammatory disease can result in scarred fallopian tubes which block the passage of a fertilized egg. The fertilized egg, therefore, cannot pass on to the uterus and the growing embryo will cause the tube to rupture. By 1990, there was a 400 percent increase in tubal pregnancies, most of which were caused by STDs. Even worse is the fact that 80 percent of those infected with an STD don't know it and will unwittingly infect their next sexual partner.

The Medical Facts of STDs

Syphilis is a terrible infection. In its first stage, the infected individual may be lulled into thinking there is little wrong since the small sore will disappear in two to eight weeks. The second and third stages are progressively worse and can eventually lead to brain, heart, and blood vessel damage if not diagnosed and treated. The saddest part is that syphilis is 100 percent curable with penicillin, yet there is more syphilis now than in the late 1940s, and it is spreading rapidly.

Chlamydia, a disease which only became common in the mid-1970s, infects 20 to 40 percent of some sexually active groups, including teenagers. In men, chlamydia is usually less serious; with females, however, the infection can be devastating. An acute chlamydia infection in women will result in pain, fever, and damage to female organs. A silent infection can damage a woman's fallopian tubes without her ever knowing it. A single chlamydia infection can result in a 25 percent chance of infertility. With a second infection, the chance of infertility rises to 50 percent. This is double the risk of gonorrhea.

The *human papilloma virus,* or HPV, is an extremely common STD. One study reported that at the University of California, Berkeley, 46 percent of the sexually active coeds were infected with HPV. Another study reported that 38 percent of the sexually active females between the ages of thirteen and twenty-one were infected. HPV is the major cause of venereal warts; it can be an extremely difficult problem to treat and may require expensive procedures such as laser surgery.

The human papilloma virus can result in precancer or cancer of the genitalia. By causing cancer of the cervix, this virus is killing more women in this country than AIDS—over forty-six hundred women in 1991. HPV can also result in painful intercourse for years after infection even though other visible signs of the disease have disappeared.

And of course there is the *HIV* virus, the virus that causes AIDS. The first few cases of AIDS were only discovered in 1981; now, in the United States alone, there are between 1 and 2 million infected with this disease. As far as we know, all of these people will die in the next ten years. As of early 1993, one hundred sixty thousand had already died.

A 1991 study at the University of Texas at Austin showed that one in one hundred students who had blood drawn for any reason at the university health center was HIV infected. While the progress of the disease is slow for many people, all who have the virus will be infected for the rest of their lives. There is no cure, and many researchers are beginning to despair of ever coming up with a cure or even a vaccine (as was eventually done with polio). In 1992, one in seventy-five men was infected with HIV and one in seven hundred women. But the number of women with AIDS is growing. In the early years of the epidemic less than 2 percent of the AIDS cases were women. Now the percentage is 12 percent.

Teenagers Face a Greater Risk from STDs

Teenagers are particularly susceptible to sexually transmitted diseases or STDs. This fact is alarming since more teens are sexually active today than ever before. An entire generation is at risk and the saddest part about it is that most of them are unaware of the dangers they face. Our teenagers must be given the correct information to help them realize that saving themselves sexually until marriage is the only way to stay healthy.

The medical reasons for teens' high susceptibility to STDs specifically relates to females. The cervix of a teenage girl has a lining that produces mucus. It is a great growth medium for viruses and bacteria. As a girl reaches her twenties or has a baby, this lining is replaced with a tougher, more resistant lining. Also during the first two years of menstruation, 50 percent of the periods occur without ovulation. This will produce a more liquid mucus which also grows bacteria and viruses very well. A fifteen-year-old girl has a one-in-eight chance of developing pelvic inflammatory disease simply by having sex, whereas a twenty-year-old woman has only a one-in-eighty chance in that situation.

Teenagers do not always respond to antibiotic treatment for pelvic inflammatory disease, and occasionally such teenage girls require a hysterectomy. Teenage infertility is also an increasing problem. In 1965, only 3.6 percent of the married couples between ages twenty and twenty-four were infertile; by 1982, that figure had nearly tripled to 10.6 percent. The infertility rate is surely higher than that now with the alarming spread of chlamydia.

Teenagers are more susceptible to human papilloma virus, HPV. Rates of HPV infection in teenagers can be as high as 40 percent, whereas in the adult population, the rate is less than 15 percent. Teenagers are also more likely than adults to develop precancerous growths as a result of HPV infection, and they are more likely to develop pelvic inflammatory disease.

Apart from the increased risk from STDs in teens, the number of teenage pregnancies is also at an unprecedented level with over 1 million pregnancies, and four hundred thousand abortions in 1985. Abortion is not a healthy procedure for anyone to undergo, especially a teenager. It is far better not to have gotten pregnant. Oral contraceptives are not as effective with teenagers, mainly because teens are more apt to forget to take the pill than adults. Over a one-year period, as many as 9 to 18 percent of teenage girls using oral contraceptives become pregnant.

Our teenagers are at great risk. In a society that has abandoned God's design for healthy meaningful sexual expression within marriage, our children need to be told the truth about the dangers of STDs.

Is "Safe Sex" the Answer?

I must now take a hard look at the message of "safe sex" which is being taught to teens at school and through the media across the country.

Some people believe that if teens can be taught how to use contraception and condoms effectively, rates of pregnancy and STD infection will be reduced dramatically. But statistics and common sense tell us otherwise. At Rutgers University, the infection rates of students with STD varied little with the form of contraception used. For example, 35 to 44 percent of the sexually active students were infected with one or more STDs whether they used no contraceptive, oral contraceptive, the diaphragm, or condoms. It is significant to note that condoms, the hero of the "safe sex" message, provided virtually no protection from STDs.

Will condoms prevent the spread of HIV, the virus that causes AIDS? While they are better than nothing, the bottom line is that condoms cannot be trusted. A study from Florida looked at couples where one individual was HIV positive and the other was negative. They used condoms as protection during intercourse. Obviously these couples would be highly motivated to use the condoms properly, yet after eighteen months, 17 percent of the previously uninfected partners were now HIV positive. That is a one-in-six chance, the same as in Russian roulette. Not good odds!

Condoms do not even provide 100 percent protection for the purpose for which they were designed: prevention of pregnancy. One study from the School of Medicine Family Planning Clinic at the University of Pennsylvania reported that 25 percent of patients using condoms as birth control over a one-year period conceived. Other studies indicate that the rate of accidental pregnancy from condom-protected intercourse is around 15 percent with married couples and 36 percent for unmarried couples.

Condoms are inherently untrustworthy. The FDA allows one in 250 to be defective. Condoms are often stored and shipped at unsafe temperatures which weakens the integrity of the latex rubber, causing breaks and ruptures. Condoms will break 8 percent of the time and slip off 7 percent of the time. There are so many pitfalls in condom use that immature teenagers can't be expected to use them properly. And even if they do, they are still at risk.

Studies are beginning to show that school-based sex education that includes condom use as the central message does not work. A study evaluating programs that emphasized condom use stated in a major pediatric journal that "the available evidence indicates that there is little or no effect from school-based sex-education on sexual activity, contraception, or teenage pregnancy."[2] Over 3 billion dollars has been spent on sex education programs emphasizing condoms with little or no effect! In addition, programs that emphasize condoms tend to give a false sense of security to sexually active students and make those students who are not having sex feel abnormal. Hardly the desired result!

The list of damaging effects from unmarried adolescent sexual activity is long indeed. Apart from the threat to physical health and fertility, there is injury to family relationships, self-confidence and emotional health, spiritual health, and future economic opportunities due to unplanned pregnancy. Condom-based sex education does not work.

The Common-Sense Solution

There is no question that the fruits of the sexual revolution, or sexual convulsion as one author put it, have been devastating. Only one message offers health, hope, and joy to today's teenagers: Save intercourse for marriage.

Sex is a wonderful gift, but if uncontrolled it has a great capacity for evil as well as good. Our bodies were not made to have multiple sex partners. Almost all risk of STD and out-of-wedlock pregnancy can be avoided by saving intercourse for marriage. And it can be done.

Statistics clearly show that in schools teaching a sex education program that emphasizes saving intercourse for marriage, the teen pregnancy rate drops dramatically in as little as one year. In San Marcos, California, a high school used a federally funded program, Teen Aid, which emphasizes saving intercourse until marriage. Before using the program there were 147 pregnancies out of six hundred girls. Within two years, the number of pregnancies plummeted to twenty out of six hundred girls.[3] In Jessup, Georgia, upon instituting the Sex Respect program, the number of pregnancies out of 340 female students dropped from seventeen to thirteen to eleven to three in successive years.

Delaying intercourse until teens are older is not a naive proposal. Over 50 percent of females and 40 percent of males ages fifteen to nineteen have not had intercourse. While not a majority, they are living proof that teens can control their sexual desires. Current condom-based sex education programs basically teach teenagers that they cannot control their sexual desires, and that they must use condoms to protect themselves. It is not a big leap from teenagers being unable to control their sexual desires to being unable to control their hate, greed, anger, and prejudice. This is not the right message for our teenagers! Teenagers are willing to discipline themselves for things they want and are convinced are beneficial. Girls get up early for drill team practice. Boys train in the off-season with weights to get stronger for athletic competition. Our teens can also be disciplined in their sexual lives if they have the right information to make logical choices. Saving sex for marriage is the common-sense solution. In fact, it is the only solution. We don't hesitate to tell our kids not to use drugs, and most do not. We tell our kids it's unhealthy to smoke, and most do not. We tell our kids not to use marijuana, and most do not.

It is normal and healthy not to have sex until marriage. Sexually transmitted diseases are so common that it is not an exaggeration to say that most people who regularly have sex outside of marriage will contract a sexually transmitted disease. Not only is saving sex for marriage the only real hope for sexual health, it is God's design. God has said that our sexuality is to blossom within the confines of a mutually faithful, monogamous relationship. What we are seeing today is the natural consequence of disobedience. We need to reeducate our kids, not just in what is best, but in what is right.

3

Sexual Purity

Ray Bohlin

As our society prepares to enter the twenty-first century, one trend and long-time staple of our culture looms ever larger on the horizon. The places to which you can escape in order to avoid sexual temptation continue to shrink. Children cannot be allowed to roam unsupervised through the neighborhood video stores because of the racks of videos with alluring covers of scantily clad exercisers and playmates of the year. The aisles of popular new releases contain images from R-rated movies that were only found in skin magazines thirty years ago. A trip to the grocery store can take you past the book aisle with suggestive covers on romance novels which contain graphic descriptions of sexual encounters. Billboards for beer, cars, and movies all use sex to sell. Radio stations readily play songs today that were banned from the airwaves decades ago. A trip to the mall takes you past stores with only sex to sell. Your home is invaded with sexually explicit images even over the free non-cable channels and your home computer. Unwelcome mail enters your home, selling well-known sex magazines that continue to earn millions of dollars every year.

From the moment Adam and Eve were ashamed of their nakedness, sexual temptation has been in our midst. But except for brief periods in declining cultures, the temptations had to be sought. There were places where one could be relatively safe from sights and sounds that inflame lust and desire. Those days are over. Oh, sure, you can have blocks installed on your computer or phone, and the local video store will allow you to put a screen on your children's rentals. But the fact that such systems are necessary and only voluntary should be enough to tell us of the pervasiveness of sex in our society. Sexual purity is a rare and often scorned virtue today. When a Hollywood couple makes it known that they are saving sex for marriage, people ask, "Why would you do that?"

While sex is clearly pervasive in our society, you don't have to look very far to find plenty of reasons to avoid sexual relations outside of marriage. The biblical words for "fornication" or "sexual immorality" refer to all sexual activity outside of marriage, and the Scriptures clearly state that all such activity is forbidden (Lev. 18; 20; Matt. 15:19; 1 Cor. 6:9–10, 18; 1 Thess. 4:3). But a person may rationalize that while sexual activity outside of marriage is sin, "I can always be forgiven for my sin, and as long as I am not found out, who gets hurt?" Paul answers this resoundingly in Romans 6. "May it never be!" cries the apostle. By allowing sin to reign in our hearts we effectively say that Christ's death and resurrection have no power in our lives.

Medical Reasons for Sexual Purity

Consider the physical consequences of sexual immorality that exist today. As observed in chapter 2, in the 1960s syphilis and gonorrhea were the only two significant sexually transmitted diseases. Today there are about twenty-five, and one in five Americans between the ages of fifteen and fifty-five has a viral STD. That number is one in four if bacterial infections are included. There are 12 million new infections every year with 60 percent of these among teenagers.

Chlamydia and gonorrhea can lead to pelvic inflammatory disease which often results in sterility. Human papilloma virus (HPV) frequently produces genital warts which can develop into cancer. Rampant HPV infection is the primary reason that women are urged to have Pap smears on a yearly basis. If you are sexually active outside of marriage and "lucky," you may only contract herpes. Even this is an embarrassing, bothersome, incurable infection. But you may get AIDS, which will kill you. Since the human immunodeficiency virus (HIV) can lie dormant for years before developing into deadly AIDS, your sex partner may not know that he or she is infected. The fact is, if you are sexually active outside of marriage, it is almost guaranteed that you will contract at least one STD.

Information is not enough. Why is sexual purity within marriage so important to God? And what do we do to avoid falling into sexual sin with so much temptation swirling around our heads? We will now turn to explore some time-tested advice from Scripture to see what we must do and why.

The Mystical Nature of Marriage

In his recent book *Reason in the Balance*, Phillip Johnson documents brilliantly the viselike grip of philosophical naturalism in science, law, and education in the United States. Our populace has been taught that matter, energy, space, and time are all that exists. Every form of cultural discourse, including our sexual behavior, has been infected. Freedom of choice and personal fulfillment are praised as the ultimate virtues because, for the naturalist, sex is just a physical act that fulfills a basic need and instinct in every person. People should be free to pursue whatever sexual expression they choose, to meet that basic physiological need. And this need is only created by our fundamental drive to reproduce and spread our genes into the next generation. In the naturalistic worldview, sex simply becomes a basic need, and marriage just a cultural expression to satisfy that need for some, but not for all people.

That is why so many people, including Christians, look at Scripture's clear statements condemning sex outside of marriage as antiquated and old-fashioned. "Oh," they say, "they applied to the people of that time, but not now. Not as we prepare to enter the twenty-first century!" But this raises some important questions. First, do the scriptural injunctions against any sex outside of marriage apply today? The answer, of course, is, "Yes, they do." We recognize readily what the Bible has to say about sex, and we see all around us the physical, emotional, and relational consequences of sexual immorality. Since God is sovereign, He erected these consequences as warning signs not to transgress His principles. But just why is sexual fidelity so important to God?

Sexual Fidelity Is Important to God

God's intentions for marriage were clearly stated right from the beginning. Genesis 2:18–25 makes it plain that God's design was for one man and one woman to stay together for life. Jesus used this passage as the basis for His teaching on divorce in Matthew 19: "What God has joined together, let man not separate" (v. 6). As Creator, God has every right to tell us what He wants.

Second, the Father has used the marriage union as an analogy for His relationship with Israel in the Old Testament and Jesus' relationship with the church in the New Testament. Isaiah 1:21, Jeremiah 2:20, 3:1–10 and especially

Ezekiel 16:15–34 accuse Israel of playing the harlot, chasing after other gods and ignoring her rightful "husband." God's union with Israel was to be forever. He was faithful, but Israel was not. The Lord rained down His judgment on the unfaithfulness of Israel and Judah. In Ephesians 5 Paul tells husbands that they are to love their wives as Christ loves the church. Elsewhere, Jesus is spoken of as the Bridegroom and the church as His bride, another relationship that is to be forever. Jesus will be faithful. Will the church? Our marital and sexual relationships are to mirror the Lord's special relationships with Israel in the Old Testament and the church in the New. God hates divorce and any sexual relationships outside of marriage, because He hates it when His faithfulness to us is spurned by our turning to other gods. This is true whether they be the pagan gods of old, which are still around, or the modern gods of self, money, power, and sex.

Well, we may know what is right, but knowing what is right is often not the same as doing what is right. Look at a passage in Proverbs that warns its readers concerning the dangers, both obvious and subtle, of sexual temptation.

A Young Man Lacking Sense Meets a Harlot

It is hard for some to imagine that the Bible contains explicit advice on how to avoid sexual temptation. But Proverbs 7 is entirely devoted to exactly that. In the first five verses Solomon pleads with his son to listen and guard his words carefully concerning the adulteress.

> *My son, keep my words,*
> *and store up my commandments within you.*
> *Keep my commandments and you will live;*

[Sounds like serious stuff!]

guard my teachings as the apple of your eye.

[Actually, the "pupil" or "little man of your eye." This was meant, therefore, to be a precious truth, closely guarded and kept.]

> *Bind them on your fingers;*
> *write them on the tablet of your heart.*
> *Say to wisdom, "You are my sister,"*
> *and call understanding your kinsman;*
> *they will keep you from the adulteress,*
> *from the wayward wife with her seductive words.*

In verses 6–9, King Solomon takes the role of an observer, telling his son what he sees unfolding before him.

> *At the window of my house*
> *I looked out through the lattice.*
> *I saw among the simple,*
> *I noticed among the young men,*
> *a youth who lacked judgment.*
> *He was going down the street near her corner,*
> *walking along in the direction of her house*
> *at twilight, as the day was fading,*
> *as the dark of night set in.*

Solomon speaks of one who is young, inexperienced, and lacking judgment. This young man purposefully walks down the street of the adulteress and actually heads straight to her house in the middle of the night. As Charlie Brown would say, "Good grief!" His intent is probably harmless. He is curious, perhaps hoping for a glimpse of her plying her wares to someone else on the street. Sin is probably not on his mind. He just wants to see what the real world is like. That kind of thinking is still heard today. "I just need to know what is out there so I can warn my family and others around me." In reality, our young fool is looking for titillation and is confident that he can withstand the temptation.

This is precisely why Solomon says he is lacking sense. The apostle Paul warns in 1 Corinthians 10:12, "So, if you think you are standing firm, be careful that you don't fall." Overconfidence is our worst enemy in the face of temptation. I am reminded of two contrasting characters in J. R. R. Tolkien's *Lord of the Rings* trilogy, Boromir and Faramir. Boromir and Faramir were brothers. Boromir, the elder, was renowned for his exploits in war. He was his father's favorite and the principal heir. He was confident, however, that were he to wield the One Ring, the Ring of Power, he would not be corrupted by it and could use it to defeat the armies of the evil Sauron. However, his overconfidence and lust for power led him to attempt to steal the ring from the designated Ring-bearer. His foolishness caused the Fellowship of the Ring to be split apart under attack and led eventually to his death. He thought he could stand, but he fell.

His brother Faramir, however, had a more realistic picture of his sinful nature. When confronted later with the same opportunity to see and even hold the ring, he refused. He knew the temptation would be strong and that the best way to resist the lust for power was to keep the temptation as far away as possible. Faramir, though perceived to be weaker than his brother, was, in a sense, actually the wiser and stronger of the two. He took heed, did not fall, and later played a significant role in the final victory over the forces of evil.

What about you? Do you consider yourself strong enough to resist the temptations presented in movies, books, commercials, and so on? Do you walk into the movie theater blindly, lacking sense, uninformed as to why this movie is rated R or even PG-13? Are you a headstrong Boromir, or a wise Faramir who knows his weakness in the face of temptation and avoids it whenever possible?

The Schemes of the Adulteress

As we continue in our walk through Proverbs 7, Solomon focuses his attention on the schemes of the seductress. Our young man lacking sense is walking down her street, right past her house. Solomon continues in verse 10: "Then out came a woman to meet him, dressed like a prostitute and with crafty intent. (She is loud and defiant, her feet never stay at home; now in the street, now in the squares, at every corner she lurks.)"

What a surprise! A woman comes to meet him! Can't you just hear Gomer Pyle exclaiming at the top of his lungs, "Surprise! Surprise! Surprise!" Surprise, indeed! This is only what was expected. Her boisterousness lends an air of fun and frivolity. Let's face it, if sin weren't so enjoyable we wouldn't fall prey to it so easily. Solomon next gives the impression that the temptress is everywhere to be found. As I pointed out earlier, that is even more true today. Even a widely proclaimed family movie like *Forrest Gump* shocked many with scenes that were unnecessary and sexually explicit. If you were surprised, you shouldn't have been. Check these things out beforehand. Don't act like a young man lacking sense and wander down the street of temptation unaware. Remember that Jesus extended the moral law from our actions to our thought life. If we simply lust after a woman, we have already committed adultery in our hearts (Matt. 5:27–28).

Solomon next turns to the woman's tactics:

She took hold of him and kissed him,

[Suddenness can put you off guard unless you have decided beforehand what you would do, whether in a situation of real seduction, watching a scene in a movie or on TV, or reading a book. Will you close your eyes, leave, change channels, skip a few pages? Know beforehand!]

And with a brazen face she said:
"I have fellowship offerings at home;
today I fulfilled my vows."

[I'm not such a bad person. See, I do a lot of the same things you do. You're not going to reject and judge me, are you?]

"So I came out to meet you;
I looked for you and have found you!"

Ah, the ultimate weapon with a man—female flattery. Men are suckers when they're told that they are needed. It was he, particularly, she was waiting for—not just anybody. If a man senses he is needed, he will be reluctant to say no. Men usually hate to disappoint. Solomon continues in verses 16–18:

"I have covered my bed with colored linens
from Egypt.
I have perfumed my bed with myrrh, aloes and
cinnamon.
Come, let's drink deep of love till morning;
let's enjoy ourselves with love!"

As she continues her assault on the male ego by indicating all the trouble she has gone through just for him ("Don't hurt my feelings now," she says), she creates a sensual picture that is meant to arouse him and draw him in. Be realistic. This sounds inviting even from the pages of Scripture. It should be a loud tornado siren in your ear telling you: "There, but for the grace of God, go I!" The adulteress finishes her seduction with the assurance that no one need ever know, in verses 19 and 20. She says: "My husband is not at home; he has gone on a long journey. He took his purse filled with money and will not be home till full moon."

This rationalization that "no one will know" is true not only of an affair, but also of what we allow into our minds through our computers, videos rented when no one else is home, magazines stashed away in a secret place, or visits to parts of town where we certainly don't expect to see acquaintances. But it's a lie. These things cannot be hidden for a lifetime. Either we will slip up sooner or later, or we will poison our minds to such an extent that the outward temptation can no longer be resisted. Moses speaks to the people of Israel in Numbers 32:23 warning them that if they do not obey the Lord, "their sin will find them out."

Facing the Consequences

As we have seen, the young man in Proverbs 7 has walked right into temptation's snare and has been totally mesmerized by the pleas and schemes of the adulteress. Now we will see the young man's demise and the consequences of his actions. We read in verses 21 through 23:

> *With persuasive words she led him astray;*
> *she seduced him with her smooth talk.*
> *All at once he followed her*

[Probably as if in a trance.]

like an ox going to the slaughter,

[Silently and dumbly.]

like a deer stepping into a noose
till an arrow pierces his liver,
like a bird darts into a snare,

[Again blindly and without knowledge.]

little knowing it will cost him his life.

He capitulates without a word, mesmerized by her seduction. The analogy to the ox, the deer, and the bird point out that each of them go blindly, silently, and unknowingly to their death. So it is with the young man lacking sense. While he will not die in a physical sense—though he may if he contracts AIDS—he will die in the sense that his life will never be the same. Not only will the shame and guilt be difficult to overcome, but there will be severed relationships that may never be repaired. There may also be consequences that can never be removed and scars that may never be healed, such as a child out of wedlock or a broken marriage in which children are the real victims. But even if his sin was with pornography, remember his sins would find him out. He might keep up appearances for a while, but his family, and his relationship with God would slowly rot from the inside out. Solomon closes chapter 7 with some final warnings and observations:

Now then, my sons, listen to me;
pay attention to what I say.
Do not let your heart turn to her ways

[Do not give your mind opportunity with impure material.]

> *or stray into her paths.*
> *Many are the victims she has brought down;*
> *her slain are a mighty throng.*
> *Her house is a highway to the grave,*
> *leading down to the chambers of death.*

Your best defense is to first realize that none are immune. Remember Boromir and Faramir from Tolkien's *Lord of the Rings*. Boromir, the stronger, older brother, thought he could resist the power of the One Ring and use it to defeat the enemy. In the end, his lust for power drove him to irrationality and eventually to his death. Faramir, however, assessed his weakness correctly and refused even to look at the ring when the opportunity arose, knowing its seductive power. He not only lived but was used mightily in the battles that followed. No one was capable of totally resisting the power of the ring. Those who actually gazed upon the ring, handled it, and used it resisted only through an extreme exercise of will often aided by the intervention and counsel of others (Bilbo, Frodo, and Samwise). Those who totally yielded to it were destroyed by it (Gollum).

Many have faltered before you and many will falter after you. Your first mistake would be to think yourself above this kind of sin or immune to it. Don't kid yourself. It can ruin you physically! It can ruin you emotionally! It can ruin you spiritually!

Purity affirms who we are; we are made in the image of God. Purity affirms our relationship to Jesus Christ as His bride. Purity affirms women as treasures God created to be companions and helpmates, not as objects to be conquered.

Pray and ask forgiveness for any involvement in pornography, R-rated movies, and lustful thoughts. Commit to decide beforehand what to do about sudden temptations. Commit to purity. Commit to be faithful to your spouse or future spouse in the power of the Holy Spirit. Martin Luther said that you cannot stop birds from flying over your head, but you can certainly stop them from making a nest in your hair. Some temptation is unavoidable, but as far as it depends on you, give it no opportunity to set up residence in your mind.

4

Why Wait Until Marriage?

Jimmy Williams
revised by Jerry Solomon

Crucial moral battles are being fought in our culture. Nowhere is this seen more vividly than in the present sexual attitudes and behavior of Americans. The average young person experiences many pressures in the formation of personal sexual standards.

The fact that some standard must be chosen cannot be ignored. Sex is here to stay, and it remains a very basic force in our lives. We cannot ignore its presence any more than we can ignore other ordinary human drives.

This chapter explores contemporary sexual perspectives within a biblical framework. Each of us needs to think through the implications of sexual alternatives and choose a personal sexual ethic based on intellectual and Christian factors, not merely on biological, emotional, or social ones.

Sex and Love

Before we begin our survey of various perspectives, we need to examine carefully the relationship of the physical act of sexual intercourse and the more intangible aspects of a meaningful relationship between two human beings.

Is having sex really making love? Modern case studies, psychological insights, church teachings, and biblical premises all seem to suggest not. As psychoanalyst Erich Fromm puts it, "To love a person productively implies to care and to feel responsible for his life, not only for his physical powers but for the growth and development of all his human powers."[1]

If sex is merely a physical thing, then masturbation or other forms of autoeroticism should provide true and complete sexual satisfaction. Such is not the case. Alternatives to normal sexual intercourse may satisfy physically, but not emotionally. Meaningful sexual activity involves the physical union of a man and a woman in a relationship of mutual caring and intimacy.

Every normal person has the physical desire for sexual activity as well as a desire to know and be known, to love and be loved. Both desires make up the real quest for intimacy in a relationship; sexual intercourse represents only one ingredient that allows us to experience true intimacy.

A superior sexual relationship exists where the bonds of mutual communication, understanding, affection, and trust have formed, and two people have committed themselves to each other in a permanent relationship. The more of these qualities that are present, the deeper the intimacy and the more meaningful the relationship. The relationship becomes more valuable as time passes because it is one of a kind—unique. To spread intimacy around through a variety of sexual liaisons destroys the accumulated value of the previous relationship(s) and dilutes and scatters (in little doses to a number of people) what one has to give.

A real challenge faces young people today. Given the choice between hamburger at five o'clock or filet mignon at seven-thirty, are there any good reasons to forego the hamburger and wait for the filet? Why not both? Why not take the hamburger now and the filet later?

This attitude is precisely the rationale of those who encourage sexual activity outside of marriage. But it is not possible to do so without encountering problems later. Too many hamburgers ruin one's taste and appreciation for filet and tend to turn filet into hamburger as well!

Arguments for Premarital Sex

Now we will begin to consider the arguments that are presented to justify sexual activity before and outside of marriage. We will analyze the arguments briefly and explore the general implications of each rationale so that you can decide which will provide the best path for your future.

Biological Argument

Perhaps the most common reason used to justify premarital sexual activity is that the sex drive is a basic biological one. The argument is as old as the Bible, where Paul states in 1 Corinthians 6:13, "Food for the stomach and the stomach for food." The Corinthians were using the biological argument to justify their immorality, but Paul explained that the analogy to the sex appetite was (and is) fallacious. Humans cannot live without food, air, or water. But we can live without sex.

Nature says several things on this point. First, God has built into the natural world a mechanism for sexual release: nocturnal emissions, or orgasmic release during dreams. Second, nature rejects human promiscuity, as the growing problem of sexually transmitted diseases makes abundantly clear.

Couples who confine sex to their marriage partners face no danger from disease. Further, we can safely conclude that abstinence does not impair one's health. Sociologist Robert Bell quips, "There appear to be no records of males hospitalized because girls refused to provide sexual outlets."[2]

While recognizing that human beings share many common characteristics with animals, we do not find comparable sexual behavioral patterns in the animal world. Human sexuality is unique in that it includes, but transcends, physical reproductive elements. It reaches an intimacy unknown among animals. Humans are different from animals.

Statistical Argument

A second popular argument reasons that everyone is doing it. First, we must categorically emphasize that this is not a true statement. A 1991 study of college freshmen shows that "about two-thirds of men (66.3 percent) and slightly more than one-third of the women (37.9 percent) support the idea of sex between people who have known each other only for a short time."[3] As sobering as such statistics may be, they obviously indicate that not everyone is sexually active.

Further, statistics do not establish moral values. Is something right because it happens frequently or because many people believe it? A primitive tribe may have a 100 percent consensus in believing that cannibalism is right! Does that make it right? A majority can be wrong. If a society sets the standards, those standards are subject to change with the whim and will of the majority. In one generation slavery may be right and abortion wrong, as in early nineteenth-century America, but in another generation, abortion is in and slavery is out, as today.

There are enough young people in any school or community who prefer to wait until marriage that the young person who wants to wait has plenty of company.[4] Each person must decide where he or she wants to be in a given statistical analysis of current sexual mores and behavior.

Proof of Love Argument

A third argument suggests that sexual activity tests or provides proof of love. Supposedly, it symbolizes how much the other cares. Pressure is therefore exerted on the more reluctant partner to demonstrate a certain level of care. Reluctant partners, succumbing to this pressure, often do so with an underlying hope that it will somehow cement the relationship and discourage the other partner from searching elsewhere for a less hesitant friend.

Any person who insists on making sex the ultimate proof of a genuine relationship isn't saying "I love you," but rather "I love it." True love concerns itself with the well-being of the other person and would not interpret sexual hesitation in such a selfish way. Furthermore, the person adopting this practice develops a pattern of demonstrating love by purely sexual responsiveness. Ultimately he or she enters marriage with something of a distortion as to what real intimacy means, to say nothing of having to deal with the memories of previous loves. Some behaviors are irreversible. The process is like trying to unscramble an egg. Once it's done, it's done.

The broader perspective sees sex as an integral and important part of a meaningful relationship, but not the totality of it. Remembering this will help an individual make the right decision to refrain from sexual involvement if a potential partner pressures to make sex the test of a meaningful relationship.

Psychological Argument

The psychological argument for premarital sex is also a popular one and is closely tied to the biological argument. Here's the question: Is sexual restraint bad for you?

Sublimating one's sex drive is not unhealthy. In

sublimation sexual and aggressive energy is displaced by nonsexual and nondestructive goals.

But guilt, unlike sublimation, can produce devastating results in humans. It is anger turned inward, producing depression, a lowered self-esteem, and fatigue. Chastity and virginity contribute very little to sexual problems. Unsatisfying relationships, guilt, hostility toward the opposite sex, and low self-esteem do. In short, there are no scars where there have been no wounds.

In this hedonistic society, some people need no further justification for sexual activity beyond the fact that it's fun. "If it feels good, do it!" says the bumper sticker. But the fun syndrome forces us to sacrifice the permanent on the altar of the immediate.

The sex act itself is no guarantee of fun. Initial sex experiences outside of marriage are often disappointing because of high anxiety and guilt levels. Fear of discovery, haste, and lack of commitment and communication all combine to spoil some of the fun. Further, there is no way to avoid the exploitation of someone in the relationship if it's just for fun. Sometimes one person's pleasure is another's pain. No one likes to be or feel used.

Marilyn Monroe was a sex symbol for millions. She said, "People took a lot for granted; not only could they be friendly, but they could suddenly get overly friendly and expect an awful lot for a very little."[5] She felt used. She died naked and alone, with an empty bottle of sleeping pills beside a silent telephone. Was the fame and fun worth it? Evidently she thought not.

Experiential Argument

This perspective emphasizes a desire on the part of an individual not to appear like a sexual novice on the wedding night. One answer to this is to have enough sexual experience prior to marriage so that one brings practice, not theory, to the initial sexual encounter in marriage. But the body was designed to perform sexually and will do so given the opportunity.

This is not to say that sexual skill cannot be gained through experience. It is to say that every skill acquired by humans must have a beginning point. If the idea of two virgins on their wedding night brings amusement to our minds instead of admiration, it is actually a sad commentary on how far we have slipped as individuals and as a culture.

It must be emphasized again that healthy sexual adjustment depends much more on communication than technique. World-famous sex therapists Masters and Johnson found: "Nothing good is going to happen in bed between a husband and wife unless good things have been happening between them before they get into bed. There is no way for a good sexual technique to remedy a poor emotional relationship."[6]

In other words, a deeply committed couple with no sexual experience is far ahead of a sexually experienced couple with a shallow and tentative commitment, as far as the marriage's future sexual success is concerned.

Compatibility Argument

A corollary to the experiential argument is the one of compatibility. The idea is, How will I know if the shoe fits unless first I try it on? A foot stays about the same size, but the human sex organs are wonderfully adaptable. A woman's vagina can enlarge to accommodate the birth of a baby or to fit a male organ of any size. Physical compatibility is 99 percent guaranteed, and the other 1 percent can become so with medical consultation and assistance.

Of greater importance is to test person-to-person compatibility. Sexual dysfunction in young people is usually psychologically based. Building bridges of love and mutual care in the nonphysical facets of the relationship are the sure roads to a honeymoon that can last a lifetime.

Contraceptive Argument

The contraceptive argument supposedly takes the fear of pregnancy out of sexual activity and gives moderns a virtual green light. Actually, the light is at most pale green and perhaps only yellow. The simple fact is that pregnancy (along with sexually transmitted diseases) remains a possibility.

Beyond the question of contraceptive use is the entire area of unwanted children. No good alternatives exist for children born out of wedlock. Do we have the right to deprive children of life or a secure family setting and loving parents to supply their basic needs? Parental love and security are highly prized. Ironically, even severely battered children choose to be with their parents over other alternatives.

Sexual intimacy between a man and a woman is not exclusively their private affair. Sexual intercourse has consequences. In sexual matters, the moral decision must come before the decision to have sex with someone, not later when unforeseen circumstances arise.

Marital Argument

Perhaps the most prominent argument for premarital sex among Christians is the one that says, "We are in love and plan to marry soon. Why should we wait?"

Dr. Howard Hendricks, an authority on the family, comments that the best way to mortgage your marriage is to play around at the door of marriage.[7] Loss of respect and intensity of feelings may occur, as well as guilt and dissatisfaction. Restraint for a time adds excitement to the relationship and makes the honeymoon something very special, not a continuation of already-established patterns. Some couples also see little value in a public declaration of marital intent. Or they may think the formality of a wedding is the equivalent of dogma. Those who prefer no public declaration but rather seek anonymity may be saying something about the depth (or lack thereof) of their commitment to one another. Do they have their fingers crossed?

Contemporary studies indicate that the marital argument is not sound. Of 100 couples who cohabit, forty break up before they marry. Of the sixty who marry, forty-five divorce —leaving only fifteen of 100 with a lasting marriage. Thus, cohabitation has two negative effects: it sharply reduces the number who marry, and dramatically increases the divorce rate of those who do.[8]

Engaged couples, according to Paul in 1 Corinthians 7:36–37, should either control their sexual drives or marry. Intercourse, then, is not proper for engaged couples. They should either keep their emotions in check or marry.

Conclusion

We have examined some of the major arguments used to justify premarital sex. If these are the strongest defenses of sex outside of marriage, the case is weak. Our brief trek through the wilderness of contemporary sexual ideas has led to some dead ends.

There are good reasons for limiting our sexual experience to the context of permanent love and care. Virginity should not be viewed as something that must be eliminated as soon as possible, but as a gift to treasure and save for a special and unique person.

The biblical standard, which puts sex within the fidelity and security of marriage, is the most responsible code that has ever been developed. You are justified in following it without apology as the best standard for protecting human, moral, and Christian values that has been devised.

The data we have discussed is not intended to condemn or produce guilt in those who may already have sexual experience outside of marriage. The good news is that Jesus Christ came for the express purpose of forgiving our sins, sexual and all others. Jesus, who is the same yesterday, today, and forever, will forgive us. The real question now is, What shall we do with the future? Christ can cleanse the past, but He expects us to respond to the light He gives us. May this discussion help you strengthen your convictions with regard to sexual decisions and behavior in the days ahead. As the adage says, today is the first day of the rest of your life.

5

Homosexuality
Questions and Answers
Sue Bohlin

Q *uestion:* Some people say homosexuality is natural and moral; others say it is unnatural and immoral. How do we know?

Answer: Our standard can only be what God says. The apostle Paul teaches, "God gave them over to shameful lusts. Even their women exchanged natural relations for unnatural ones. In the same way the men also abandoned natural relations with women and were inflamed with lust for one another. Men committed indecent acts with other men, and received in themselves the due penalty for their perversion" (Rom. 1:26–27).

So even though homosexual desires may feel natural, they are actually unnatural, because God says they are. He also calls all sexual involvement outside of marriage immoral. (There are forty-four references to fornication—sexual immorality—in the Bible.) Therefore, any form of homosexual activity, a one-night stand or a long-term monogamous relationship, is by definition immoral, just as any abuse of heterosexuality outside of marriage is immoral.

Question: Is homosexuality an orientation God intended for some people, or is it a perversion of normal sexuality?

Answer: If God had intended homosexuality to be a viable sexual alternative for some people, He would not have condemned it as an abomination. It is never mentioned in Scripture in anything but negative terms, and nowhere does the Bible even hint at approving or giving instruction for homosexual relationships. Some theologians have argued that David and Jonathan's relationship was a homosexual one, but this claim has no basis in Scripture. David and Jonathan's deep friendship was not sexual; it was one of godly emotional intimacy that truly glorified the Lord.

Homosexuality is a manifestation of the sinful nature that all people share. At the fall of man (Gen. 3), God's perfect creation was spoiled, and the taint of sin affected us physically, emotionally, intellectually, spiritually—and sexually. Homosexuality is a perversion of heterosexuality, which is God's plan for His creation. The Lord Jesus said, "At the beginning the Creator 'made them male and female,' and said, 'For this reason a man will leave his father and mother and be united to his wife, and the two will become one flesh' " (Matt. 19:4–5).

Homosexual activity and premarital or extramarital heterosexual activity are all sinful attempts to find sexual and emotional expression in ways God never intended. God's desire for the person caught in the trap of homosexuality is the same as for every other person caught in the trap of the sin nature—that we submit every area of our lives to Him and be transformed from the inside out by the renewing of our minds.

Question: What causes a homosexual orientation?

Answer: This is a complex issue, and it is unfair to give simplistic answers or explanations. Some people start out as heterosexuals, but they rebel against God with such passionate self-indulgence that they end up embracing the gay lifestyle as another form of sexual expression. As one entertainer put it, "I'm not going to go through life with one arm tied behind my back!"

But the majority of gays sense they are "different" from very early in life, and at some point they are encouraged to identify this difference as being gay. These people may be the victims of "preconditions" that dispose them toward homosexuality. One such precondition may be a genetic predisposition for homosexuality. Although their work is far from conclusive, researchers such as Simon LeVay, Michael Bailey, and Richard Pillard have argued that homosexual tendencies may be indicated even before birth. Another precondition is the presence of childhood abuse, either emotional or sexual. It is very difficult to find a homosexual who did not experience the trauma of intense rejection, the horror of being molested, or the shock of an early sexual experience.

Question: Wouldn't the presence of preconditions let homosexuals "off the hook," so to speak?

Answer: Preconditions make it easier to sin in a particular area. They do not excuse the sin. We can draw a parallel with alcoholism. Alcoholics often experience a genetic or environmental precondition, which makes it easier for them to fall into the sin of drunkenness. Is it a sin to want a drink? No. It's a sin to drink to excess.

All of us experience various predispositions that make it easier for us to fall into certain sins. For example, highly intelligent people find it easier to fall into the sin of intellectual pride. People who were physically abused as children may fall into the sins of rage and violence more easily than others.

Current popular thinking says that our behavior is determined by our environment or our genes, or both. But the Bible gives us the dignity and responsibility missing from that mechanistic view of life. God has invested us with free will—the ability to make real, significant choices. We can choose our responses to the influences on our lives, or we can choose to let them control us.

If there is either a genetic or environmental predisposition for homosexuality, a person with this condition will fall into the sin of the gay lifestyle much more easily than a person without it will. But each of us alone is responsible for giving ourselves permission to cross over from temptation into sin.

Question: What's the difference between homosexual temptation and sin?

Answer: Unasked for, uncultivated sexual desires for a person of the same sex constitute temptation, not sin. Since the Lord Jesus was "tempted in every way, just as we are," He fully knows the intensity and nature of homosexual temptations. But He never gave in to them.

The line between sexual temptation and sexual sin is the same for both heterosexuals and homosexuals. It is the point at which our conscious thoughts will get involved. Sin begins with the internal acts of lusting and creating sexual fantasies. Lust is indulging your sexual desires by deliberately choosing to feed sexual attraction—you might say it is the sinful opposite of meditation. Sexual fantasies are conscious acts of the imagination. They are the creation of mental pornographic home movies. As the Lord said in the Sermon on the Mount, all sexual sin starts in the mind long before it gets to the point of physical expression.

Many homosexuals claim, "I never asked for these feelings. I did not choose them," and this may be true. That is why it is significant to note that the Bible specifically condemns homosexual practices, but not undeveloped homosexual feelings (temptation). There is a difference between having sexual feelings and letting them grow into lust.

Question: Isn't it true that "once gay, always gay?"

Answer: It is certainly true that most homosexuals never become heterosexual—some because they don't want to, but most others because their efforts to change were unsuccessful. It takes spiritual submission and emotional work to repent of sexual sin and to seek a healthy self-concept that glorifies God.

But for the person caught in the trap of homosexual desires who wants sexual and emotional wholeness, there is hope in Christ. In addressing the church at Corinth, the apostle Paul lists an assortment of deep sins, including homosexual offenses. He says, "And that is what some of you were. But you were washed, you were sanctified, you were justified in the name of the Lord Jesus Christ" (1 Cor. 6:11).

The Lord's loving redemption includes eventual freedom from all sin that is yielded to Him. Some people experience no homosexual temptations ever again. But for most others who are able to achieve change, homosexual desires are gradually reduced from a major problem to a minor nuisance that no longer dominates their lives. The probability of heterosexual desires returning or emerging depends on a person's sexual history.

But the potential for heterosexuality is present in everyone because God put it there.

Question: If homosexuality is such an abomination to God, why doesn't it disappear when someone becomes a Christian?

Answer: When we are born again, we bring with us all of our emotional needs and all of our old ways of relating. Homosexuality is a relational problem of meeting emotional needs the wrong way; it is not an isolated problem of mere sexual preference. With the power of the indwelling Spirit, a Christian can cooperate with God to change this unacceptable part of life. Some people—a very few—are miraculously delivered from homosexual struggles. But for the majority, real change is slow. As in dealing with any besetting sin, it is a process, not an event. Sin's power over us is broken at the moment we are born again, but learning to depend on the Holy Spirit to say no to sin and yes to godliness takes time. Second Corinthians 3:18 says, "We . . . are being transformed into his likeness with ever-increasing glory." Transformation (this side of eternity!) is a process that takes awhile. Life in a fallen world is a painful struggle. It is not a pleasant thing to have two oppositional natures at war within us!

Homosexuality is not one problem; it is symptomatic of other, deeper problems involving emotional needs and an unhealthy self-concept. Salvation is only the beginning of emotional health. It allows us to experience human intimacy as God intended us to, finding healing for our damaged emotions. It isn't that faith in Christ isn't enough; faith in Christ is the beginning.

Question: Does the fact that I had an early homosexual experience mean I'm gay?

Answer: Sex is strictly meant for adults. The Song of Songs says three times, "Do not arouse or awaken love until it so desires" (2:7; 3:5; 8:4). This is a warning not to raise sexual feelings until the time is right. Early sexual experience can be painful or pleasurable, but either way, it constitutes child abuse. It traumatizes a child. This loss of innocence does need to be addressed and perhaps even grieved through, but it doesn't mean you're gay.

Even apart from the sexual aspect, though, our culture has come to view close friendships with a certain amount of suspicion. If you enjoy emotional intimacy with a friend of the same sex, especially if it is accompanied by the presence of sexual feelings that emerge in adolescence, you can find yourself very confused. But it doesn't mean you're gay.

Sometimes young people engage in sexual experimentation, including homosexual encounters. It is a tragic myth that once a person has a homosexual experience, or even thinks about one, that he or she is gay for life.

Question: Are homosexuals condemned to hell?

Answer: Homosexuality is not a "heaven or hell" issue. The only determining factor is whether a person has been reconciled to God through Jesus Christ.

In 1 Corinthians 6, Paul says that homosexual offenders and a whole list of other sinners will not inherit the kingdom of God. But then he reminds the Corinthians that they have been washed, sanctified, and justified in Jesus' name. Paul makes a distinction between unchristian behavior and Christian behavior. He's saying, "You're not pagans anymore, you are a holy people belonging to King Jesus. Now act like it!"

If homosexuality doesn't send anyone to hell, then can the believer indulge in homosexual behavior, safe in his or her eternal security? As Paul said, "May it never be!" If someone is truly a child of God, he or she cannot continue sinful behavior that offends and grieves the Father without suffering the consequences. God disciplines those He loves.

Question: How do I respond when someone in my life tells me he or she is gay?

Answer: Take your cue from the Lord Jesus. He didn't avoid sinners; He ministered grace and compassion to them— without ever compromising His commitment to holiness. Start by cultivating a humble heart, especially concerning the temptation to react with judgmental condescension. As Billy Graham said, "Never take credit for not falling into a temptation that never tempted you in the first place."

Seek to understand your gay friend's feelings. Is this person comfortable with his gayness, or bewildered and resentful of it? Understanding people doesn't mean that you have to agree with them—but it is the best way to minister grace and love in a difficult time. Accept the fact that, to this person, these feelings are normal. You can't change his mind or feelings. Too often, parents will send their gay child to a counselor and say, "Fix him." It just doesn't work that way.

As a Christian, you are a light shining in a dark place. Be a friend with a tender heart and a winsome spirit; the biggest problem of homosexuals is not their sexuality, but their need for Jesus Christ. At the same time, predecide what your boundaries will be for behavior you just cannot condone in your presence. One college student I know excuses herself from a group when the affection becomes physical; she just gets up and leaves. It is all right to be uncomfortable around blatant sin; you do not have to subject yourself—and the Holy Spirit within you—to what grieves Him. Consider how you would be a friend to people who are living promiscuous heterosexual lives. Like the Lord, we need to value and esteem the person without condoning the sin.

Resources

Aardweg, Gerard Can Den. *Homosexuality and Hope.* Ann Arbor, Mich.: Servant, 1985.

Arterburn, Jerry. *How Will I Tell My Mother?* Nashville: Oliver Nelson, 1989.

Comiskey, Andy. *Pursuing Sexual Wholeness.* Lake Mary, Fla.: Creation House, 1989.

Consiglio, William. *Homosexual No More.* Wheaton, Ill.: Victor, 1991.

Dallas, Joe. *Desires in Conflict.* Eugene, Ore.: Harvest House, 1991. (Particularly good!)

Konrad, J. A. *You Don't Have to Be Gay.* Newport Beach, Calif.: Pacific, 1987.

Moberly, Elizabeth. *Homosexuality: A New Christian Ethic.* Greenwood, S.C.: Attic, 1983.

6

Homosexual Myths

Sue Bohlin

In this chapter we'll be looking at some of the homosexual myths that have pervaded our culture and answering their arguments. Much of this material is taken from Joe Dallas's excellent book, *A Strong Delusion: Confronting the "Gay Christian" Movement.*[1] While this chapter may prove helpful, it is our prayer that you will be able to share the facts calmly and compassionately, remembering that homosexuality isn't just a political and moral issue; it is also about people who are badly hurting. Let's consider some of the myths about homosexuality.

Myth 1: Ten percent of the population is homosexual.

In 1948, Dr. Alfred Kinsey released a study called "Sexual Behavior in the Human Male," claiming that between 10 and 47 percent of the male population was homosexual.[2] He got his figures from a pool of 5,300 male subjects that he represented as average "Joe College" students. Many of the men who gave him the data, though, actually consisted of sex offenders, prisoners, pimps, hold-up men, thieves, male prostitutes and other criminals, and hundreds of gay activists.[3] The 10 percent figure was widely circulated by Harry Hay, the father of the homosexual "civil rights" movement, urging that homosexuality be seen no longer as an act of sodomy but as a 10 percent minority class.[4]

Kinsey's figures were exposed as completely false immediately afterward, and by many other scientists since. The actual figure is closer to 2 to 3 percent.[5] But the 10 percent number has been so often reported in the press that most people think it's valid. It's not.

Myth 2: People are born gay.

Ann Landers said it, and millions of people believe it. The problem is, the data's not there to support it. There are three ways to test for inborn traits: twin studies, brain dissections, and gene "linkage" studies.[6] Twin studies show that something other than genetics must account for homosexuality, because nearly half of the identical twins studied didn't have the same sexual preference. If homosexuality were inherited, identical twins should either be both straight or both gay. Besides, none of the twin studies have been replicated, and other twin studies have produced completely different results.[7]

Dr. Simon LeVay's famous study on the brains of dead subjects yielded questionable results regarding its accuracy. He wasn't sure of the sexual orientation of the people in the study, and Dr. LeVay even admits he doesn't know if the changes in the brain structures were the cause *of* homosexuality or caused *by* homosexuality.[8]

Finally, an early study attempting to show a link between homosexuality and the X-chromosome has yet to be replicated, and a second study actually contradicted the findings of the first.[9] Even if homosexuality were someday proven to be genetically related, *inborn* does not necessarily mean *normal.* Some children are born with cystic fibrosis, but that doesn't make it a normal condition.

Inborn tendencies toward certain behaviors (such as homosexuality) do not make those behaviors moral. Tendencies toward alcoholism, obesity, and violence are now thought to be genetically influenced, but they are not good behaviors. People born with tendencies toward these behaviors have to fight hard against their natural temptations to drunkenness, gluttony, and physical rage.

And since we are born as sinners into a fallen world, we have to deal with the consequences of the Fall. Just because we're born with something doesn't mean it's normal. It's not true that "God makes some people gay." All of us have effects of the Fall we need to deal with.

Myth 3: Nothing is wrong in the marriage of people who love and are committed to each other, regardless of their respective genders.

There are two aspects to marriage: the legal and the spiritual. Marriage is more than a social convention, more than being best friends with somebody, because heterosexual marriage usually results in the production of children. Marriage is a legal institution that offers protection for women and children. Women need the freedom to devote their time and energy to nurturing and caring for their children without being forced to be breadwinners as well. God's plan is for children to grow up in families who provide for them, protect them, and wrap them in security.

Because gay or lesbian couples are by nature unable to reproduce, they do not need the legal protection of marriage to provide a safe place for the production and raising of children. Apart from the sexual aspect of a gay relationship, what they have is really "best friend" status, and that does not require legal protection.

Of course, a growing number of gay couples are seeking to have a child together, either by adoption, artificial insemination, or surrogate mothering. Despite the fact that they are able to resort to an outside procedure in order to become parents, the presence of adults plus children in an ad hoc household should not automatically secure official recognition of their relationship as a family. A movement in our culture seeks to redefine "family" any way it wants, but with a profound lack of discernment about the long-term effects on the people involved. Gay parents are making a dangerous statement to their children: lesbian mothers are saying that fathers are not important, and homosexual fathers are saying that mothers are not important. More and more social observers see the importance of both fathers and mothers in children's lives; one of their roles is to teach boys what it means to be a boy and girls what it means to be a girl.

The other aspect of marriage is of a spiritual nature. Granted, this response to the gay marriage argument won't make any difference to people who are unconcerned about spiritual things, but there are a lot of gays who care very deeply about God and long for a relationship with Him. The marriage relationship, including its emotional and especially its sexual components, is designed to serve as an earthbound illustration of the relationship between Christ and His bride, the church.[10]

Just as there is a mystical oneness between a man and a woman, who are very different from each other, so there is a mystical unity between two very different, very "other" beings—the eternal Son of God and us mortal, creaturely humans. Marriage, as God designed it, is like the almost improbable union of butterfly and buffalo, or fire and water. But homosexual relationships are the coming to-gether of two like individuals; the dynamic of unity and diversity in heterosexual marriage is completely missing, and therefore so is the spiritual dimension that is so intrinsic to the purpose of marriage. Both on an emotional and a physical level, the sameness of male and male, or female and female, demonstrates that homosexual relationships do not reflect the spiritual parable that marriage is meant to be. God wants marriage partners to complement, not to mirror, each other. The concept of gay marriage doesn't work, whether we look at it on a social level or a spiritual one.

Myth 4: Jesus said nothing about homosexuality.

Whether from a pulpit or at a gay rights event, gay activists like to point out that Jesus never addressed the issue of homosexuality; instead, they say, He was more interested in love. Their point is that if Jesus didn't spe-cifically forbid a behavior, then who are we to judge those who engage in it?

This argument assumes that the Gospels are more im-portant than the rest of the books in the New Testament, that only the recorded sayings of Jesus matter. But John's gospel itself assures us that it is not an exhaustive record of all that Jesus said and did, which means there was a lot left out![11] The Gospels don't record that Jesus condemned wife-beating or incest; does that make them okay? Fur-thermore, the remaining books of the New Testament are no less authoritative than the Gospels. All Scripture is inspired by God, not just the books with red letters in the text. Specific prohibitions against homosexual behavior in Romans 1:26–27 and 1 Corinthians 6:9–10 are every bit as God-ordained as what is recorded in the Gospels.

We do know, however, that Jesus spoke in specific terms about God's created intent for human sexuality: "At the beginning the Creator 'made them male and female,' and said, 'For this reason a man will leave his father and mother and be united to his wife, and the two will become one flesh.' . . . Therefore what God has joined together, let man not separate" (Matt. 19:4–6). God's plan is holy heterosexuality, and Jesus spelled it out.

The Levitical laws against homosexual behavior are not valid today. Leviticus 18:22 says, "Do not lie with a man as one lies with a woman; that is detestable." Gay theologians argue that the term "abomination" is generally associated with idolatry and the Canaanite religious practice of cult prostitution, and thus God did not prohibit the kind of homosexuality we see today.

Other sexual sins such as adultery and incest are also prohibited in the same chapters where the prohibitions against homosexuality are found. All sexual sin is forbidden by both the Old and New testaments completely apart from the Levitical codes, because it is a moral issue. It is true that we are not bound by the rules and rituals in Leviticus that marked Yahweh's people by their separation from the world; however, the nature of sexual sin has not changed because immorality is an affront to the holiness and purity of God Himself. Just because most of Leviticus doesn't apply to Christians today doesn't mean none of it does.

The argument that the word translated "detestable" is connected with idolatry is well answered by examining Proverbs 6:16–19, which describes what else the Lord considers detestable: a proud look, a lying tongue, hands that shed innocent blood, a heart that devises evil imaginations, feet that are swift in running to mischief, a false witness that speaks lies, and a man who sows discord among brothers. Idolatry plays no part in these abominations. The argument doesn't hold water.

If the practices in Leviticus 18 and 20 are condemned because of their association with idolatry, then it logically follows that they would be permissible if they were committed apart from idolatry. That would mean incest, adultery, bestiality, and child sacrifice (all of which are listed in these chapters) are only condemned when associated with idolatry; otherwise, they are allowable. No responsible reader of these passages would agree with such a premise.[12]

> Myth 5: Calling homosexuality a sin is judging, and judging is a sin.

Josh McDowell says that the most often-quoted Bible verse used to be John 3:16, but now that tolerance has become the ultimate virtue, the verse we hear quoted the most is "Judge not, that ye be not judged" (Matt. 7:1 KJV). The person who calls homosexual activity wrong is called a bigot and a homophobe, and even those who don't believe in the Bible can be heard to quote the "judge not" verse.

When Jesus said, "Do not judge, or you too will be judged," the context makes it plain that He was talking about setting ourselves up as judge of another person, while blind to our own sinfulness. There's no doubt about it, there is a grievous amount of self-righteousness in the way the church treats those struggling with the temptations of homosexual longings. But there is a difference between agreeing with the standard of Scripture when it declares homosexuality wrong and personally condemning an individual because of his sin. Agreeing with God about something isn't necessarily judging.

Imagine I'm speeding down the highway, and I get

pulled over by a police officer. He approaches my car and, after checking my license and registration, he says, "You broke the speed limit back there, ma'am." Can you imagine a citizen indignantly leveling a politically correct charge at the officer: "Hey, you're judging me! 'Judge not, that ye not be judged!'" The policeman is simply pointing out that I broke the law. He's not judging my character; he's comparing my behavior to the standard of the law. It's not judging when we restate what God has said about His moral law, either. What is sin is to look down our noses at someone who falls into a sin different from ours. That's judging.

> Myth 6: Romans 1 does not describe true homosexuals, but heterosexuals who indulge in homosexual behavior.

Romans 1:26–27 says, "God gave them over to shameful lusts. Even their women exchanged natural relations for unnatural ones. In the same way the men also abandoned natural relations with women and were inflamed with lust for one another. Men committed indecent acts with other men, and received in themselves the due penalty for their perversion." Some gay theologians try to get around the clear prohibition against both gay and lesbian homosexuality by explaining that the real sin Paul is talking about here is straight people who indulge in homosexual acts, because it's not natural to them. Homosexuality, they maintain, is not a sin for true homosexuals.

But nothing in this passage suggests a distinction between "true" homosexuals and "false" ones. Paul describes the homosexual behavior itself as unnatural, regardless of who commits it. In fact, he chooses unusual words for men and women, Greek words that most emphasize the biology of being a male and a female. The behavior described in this passage is unnatural for males and females; sexual orientation isn't the issue at all. He is saying that homosexuality is biologically unnatural—not just unnatural to heterosexuals, but unnatural to anyone.

Furthermore, Romans 1 describes men "inflamed with lust" for one another. This would hardly seem to indicate men who were straight by nature but experimenting with gay sex.[13] You really have to do some mental gymnastics to make Romans 1 say anything other than all homosexual activity is sin.

Myth 7: Preaching against homosexuality causes gay teenagers to commit suicide.

I received an e-mail from someone who assured me that the blood of gay teenagers was on my hands because saying that homosexuality is wrong makes people kill themselves. The belief that gay teenagers are at high risk for suicide is largely inspired by a 1989 report by a special federal task force on youth and suicide. This report stated three things: (1) gay and lesbian youths account for one third of all teenage suicides; (2) suicide is the leading cause of death among gay teenagers; (3) gay teens who commit suicide do so because of "internalized homophobia" and violence directed at them.[14] This report has been cited over and over in both gay and mainstream publications.

San Francisco gay activist Paul Gibson wrote this report based on research so shoddy that when it was submitted to Dr. Louis Sullivan, the former Secretary of Health and Human Services, Dr. Sullivan officially distanced himself and his department from it.[15] The report's numbers, both in its data and its conclusions, are extremely questionable. Part of the report cites an author claiming that as many as three thousand gay youths kill themselves each year. But that's over a thousand more than the total number of teen suicides in the first place! Gibson exaggerated his numbers when he said that one third of all teen suicides are committed by gay youth. He got this figure by looking at gay surveys taken at drop-in centers for troubled teens, many of whom were gay oriented. They revealed that gay teens had two to four times the suicidal tendencies of straight kids. Gibson multiplied this higher figure by the disputed Kinsey figure of a 10 percent homosexual population to produce his figure that 30 percent of all youth suicides are gay. David Shaffer, a Columbia University psychiatrist who specializes in teen suicides, pored over this study and said, "I struggled for a long time over Gibson's mathematics, but in the end, it seemed more hocus-pocus than math."[16]

The report's conclusions are contradicted by other, more credible reports. Researchers at the University of California in San Diego interviewed the survivors of 283 suicides for a 1986 study. Of those who died, 133 were under thirty, and only 7 percent were gay. They were all over twenty-one years old. In another study at Columbia University, of 107 teenage boy suicides, only three were known to be gay, and two of those died in a suicide pact. When the Gallup organization interviewed almost seven hundred teenagers who knew a teen who had committed suicide, not one mentioned sexuality as part of the problem. Those who had come close to killing themselves mainly cited boy-girl problems or low self-esteem.[17]

Gibson didn't use a heterosexual control group in his study. Conclusions and statistics are bound to be skewed without a control group. When psychiatrist David Shaffer examined the case histories of the gay teens who committed suicide in Gibson's report, he found the same issues that straight kids wrestle with before suicide: "The stories were the same: a court appearance scheduled for the day of the death; prolonged depression; drug and alcohol problems; etc."[18]

That any teenager should experience so much pain that he takes his life is a tragedy, regardless of the reason. But it's not fair to lay the responsibility for gay suicides, the few that there are, on those who agree with God that homosexuality is wrong and harmful behavior.

Part 2
Social Issues

Divorce

Kerby Anderson

F amilies are experiencing many problems today, but the role of divorce in this picture has been frequently overlooked because its destructive effects have been subtle, though insidious. When the divorce rate increased in the 1960s, few would have predicted its dire consequences three decades later. Yet divorce has changed both the structure and the impact of the family.

This is not just the conclusion of Christians, but also the conclusion of non-Christian researchers working in the field. Clinical psychologist Diane Medved set out to write a book to help couples facing transitions due to divorce. She begins her book with this startling statement:

> I have to start with a confession: This isn't the book I set out to write. I planned to write something consistent with my previous professional experience helping people with decision making. . . . For example, I started this project believing that people who suffer over an extended period in unhappy marriages ought to get out. . . . I thought that striking down taboos about divorce was another part of the ongoing enlightenment of the

women's, civil-rights, and human potential
movements of the last twenty-five years. . . .
To my utter befuddlement, the extensive
research I conducted for this book brought
me to one inescapable and irrefutable conclusion: I had been wrong.[1]

She titled her book *The Case Against Divorce.*

Until the 1960s, divorce had been a relatively rare phenomenon. Certainly there have always been some couples
who have considered divorce an option. But fundamental
changes in our society in the last few decades have changed
divorce from being rare to routine.

During the 1970s, the divorce rate doubled (and the
number of divorces tripled from four hundred thousand in
1962 to 1.2 million in 1981).[2] The increase in the divorce
rate came not from older couples but from the baby boom
generation. One sociologist at Stanford University calculated
that while men and women in their twenties comprised only
about 20 percent of the population, they contributed 60
percent of the growth in the divorce rate in the 1960s and
early 1970s.[3]

This increase was due to at least two major factors:
attitude and opportunity. The baby boom generation's attitude toward such issues as fidelity, chastity, and commitment were strikingly different from their parents'. Their
parents would stay in a marriage in order to make it work.
Baby boomers, however, were less committed to the ideal
of marriage and quite willing to end what they felt was a
bad marriage and move on with their lives. While their
parents might keep a marriage going "for the sake of the
kids," the baby boom generation as a whole was much less
concerned about such issues.

Economic opportunities also seem to be a significant factor in divorce. The rise in divorce closely parallels the increase in the number of women working. Women with paychecks were less likely to stay in a marriage that wasn't fulfilling to them. Armed with a measure of economic power, many women had less incentive to stay in a marriage and work out their differences with their husbands. A study of mature women done at Ohio State University found that the higher a woman's income in relation to the total income of her family, the more likely she was to seek a divorce.[4]

Divorce and Children

Divorce is having a devastating impact on both adults and children. Every year, parents of over a million children divorce. These divorces effectively cut one generation off from another. Children are reared without the presence of either their father or their mother. Children are often forced to take sides in the conflict. And, children often carry the scars of the conflict and frequently blame themselves for the divorce.

So what is the impact? Well, one demographer looking at this ominous trend of divorce and, reflecting on its impact, acknowledged: "No one knows what effect divorce and remarriage will have on the children of the baby boom. A few decades ago, children of divorced parents were an oddity. Today they are the majority. The fact that divorce is the norm may make it easier for children to accept their parents' divorce. But what will it do to their marriages in the decades ahead? No one will know until it's too late to do anything about it."[5]

What little we do know about the long-term impact of divorce is disturbing. In 1971, Judith Wallerstein began a study of sixty middle-class families in the midst of divorce. Her ongoing research has provided a longitudinal study of the long-term effects of divorce on parents and children.

Like Diane Medved, Judith Wallerstein had to revise her previous assumptions. According to the prevailing view at the time, divorce was seen as a brief crisis that would resolve itself. Her book, *Second Chances: Men, Women and Children a Decade After Divorce,* vividly illustrates the long-term psychological devastation wrought not only on the children but the adults.[6] Here are just a few of her findings in her study of the aftershocks of divorce:

- Three out of five children felt rejected by at least one parent.
- Five years after their parents' divorce, more than one-third of the children were doing markedly worse than they had been before the divorce.
- Half of the children grew up in settings in which the parents were warring with each other even after the divorce.
- One-third of the women and one-quarter of the men felt that life was unfair, disappointing, and lonely.

In essence, Wallerstein found that the emotional tremors register on the psychological Richter scale many years after the divorce.

In addition to the emotional impact is the educational impact. Children growing up in broken homes do not do as well in school as children from stable families. One national study found an overall average of one lost year of education for children in single-parent families.[7]

Divorce and remarriage adds a twist to modern families. Nearly half of all marriages in 1990 involved at least one person who had been down the aisle before—up from 31 percent in 1970.[8]

These changing family structures complicate relationships. Divorce and remarriage shuffle family members together in foreign and awkward ways. Clear lines of authority and communication get blurred and confused in these newly revised families. One commentator trying to get a linguistic handle on these arrangements called them "neo-nuclear" families.[9] The rules for these "neo-nukes" are complex and ever changing. Children looking for stability are often insecure and frustrated. One futuristic commentator imagined this possible scenario:

> On a spring afternoon, half a century from today, the Joneses are gathered to sing "Happy Birthday" to Junior. There's Dad and his third wife, Mom and her second husband, Junior's two half brothers from his father's first marriage, his six stepsisters from his mother's spouse's previous unions, 100-year-old Great Grandpa, all eight of Junior's current "grand-parents," assorted aunts, uncles-in-law and step-cousins. While one robot scoops up the gift wrappings and another blows out the candles, Junior makes a wish . . . that he didn't have so many relatives.[10]

The stress on remarried couples is difficult enough, but it intensifies when stepchildren are involved. Conflict between a step-parent and stepchild is inevitable and can be enough to threaten the stability of a remarriage. According to one study, remarriages that involve stepchildren are more likely to end in divorce than those that don't.[11]

Fully 17 percent of marriages that are remarriages for both husband and wife, and that involve stepchildren, break up within three years.[12]

No-Fault Divorce

Historically the laws governing marriage were based upon the traditional, Judeo-Christian belief that marriage was for life. Marriage was intended to be a permanent institution. Thus, the desire for divorce was not held to be self-justifying. Legally the grounds for divorce had to be circumstances that justified making an exemption to the assumption of marital permanence. The spouse seeking a divorce had to prove that the other spouse had committed one of the "faults" recognized as justifying the dissolution of the marriage. In most states, the classic grounds for divorce were cruelty, desertion, and adultery.

This legal foundation changed when California enacted a statute in 1969 which allowed for no-fault divorce. This experiment has effectively led to what could now be called "divorce on demand." One by one, various state legislatures enacted no-fault divorce laws so that today, this concept has become the *de facto* legal principle in every state.

The fault-based system of divorce law had its roots in the view that marriage was a sacrament and indissoluble. The current no-fault provisions changed this perception. Marriage is no longer viewed as a covenant; it's a contract. But it's an even less reliable contract than a standard business contract.

Classic contract law holds that a specific promise is binding and cannot be broken merely because the promisor changes his or her mind. In fact, the concept of "fault" in divorce proceedings is more like tort law than contract law in that it implies a binding obligation between two parties which has been breached, thus leading to a divorce.

When state legislatures implemented no-fault divorce provisions, they could have replaced the fault-based protections with contract-like protections. Unfortunately, they did not. In just a few decades we have moved from a position in which divorce was permitted for a few reasons to a position in which divorce is permitted for any reason, or no reason at all.

The impact on the institution of marriage has been devastating. Marginal marriages are much easier to dissolve, and couples who might have tried to stick it out and work out their problems instead opt for a no-fault divorce.

But all marriages (not just marginal marriages) are at risk. After all, marriages do not start out marginal. Most marriages start out on a solid footing. But after the honeymoon comes the more difficult process of learning to live together harmoniously. The success of the process is affected by both internal factors (willingness to meet each other's needs, and so on) and external factors (such as the availability of divorce). But even these factors are interrelated. If the law gives more protection to the marriage contract, a partner may be more likely to love sacrificially and invest effort in the marriage. If the law gives less protection, a partner may be more likely to adopt a "looking out for number one" attitude.

Biblical Perspective

The Bible speaks to the issue of divorce in both the Old Testament and the New Testament. The most important Old Testament passage on divorce is Deuteronomy 24:1–4.

> If a man marries a woman who becomes displeasing to him because he finds something indecent about her, and he writes her a certificate of divorce, gives it to her and

> sends her from his house, and if after she leaves his house she becomes the wife of another man, and her second husband dislikes her and writes her a certificate of divorce, gives it to her and sends her from his house, or if he dies, then her first husband, who divorced her, is not allowed to marry her again after she has been defiled. That would be detestable in the eyes of the LORD. Do not bring sin upon the land the LORD your God is giving you as an inheritance.

These verses were not intended to endorse divorce, just the contrary. The intention was to regulate the existing custom of divorce, not to put forth God's ideal for marriage. Divorce was allowed in certain instances because of human sinfulness (Matt. 19:8).

Divorce was widespread in the ancient Near East. The certificate of divorce apparently was intended to protect the reputation of the woman and provided her with the right to remarry. This public declaration protected her from charges of adultery. The Mishnah, for example, stated that a divorce certificate was not valid unless the husband explicitly said, "Thou art free to marry any man."[13]

Key to understanding this passage is the definition of "something indecent." It probably did not mean adultery since that was subject to the penalty of death (Deut. 22:22), nor premarital intercourse with another man (22:20-21) since that carried the same penalty. The precise meaning of the phrase is unknown.

In fact, the meaning of this phrase was subject to some debate even during the time of Christ. The conservative school of Shammai understood it to mean a major sexual

offense. The liberal school of Hillel taught that it referred
to anything displeasing to the husband (including something as trivial as spoiling his food). The apparent purpose
of this law was to prevent frivolous divorce and to protect
a woman who was divorced by her husband. The passage
in no way encourages divorce but regulates the consequences of divorce.

Another significant Old Testament passage is Malachi
2:10–16.

> Have we not all one Father? Did not one
> God create us? Why do we profane the
> covenant of our fathers by breaking faith
> with one another? . . . Has not the Lord
> made them one? In flesh and spirit they are
> his. And why one? Because he was seeking
> godly offspring. So guard yourself in your
> spirit, and do not break faith with the wife
> of your youth. "I hate divorce," says the
> Lord God of Israel.

This passage deals with breaking a prior agreement or
covenant. It specifically addresses the issue of illegal inter-
marriage and the issue of divorce. Malachi teaches that
husbands and wives are to be faithful to one another because
they have God as their Father. The marriage relationship
is built upon a solemn covenant. While God may tolerate
divorce under some of the circumstances described in
Deuteronomy 24, the instructions were given to protect
the woman if a divorce should occur. This passage in
Malachi reminds us that God hates divorce.

In the New Testament book of Matthew, we have the
clearest teachings by Jesus on the subject of divorce.

> It has been said, "Anyone who divorces his
> wife must give her a certificate of divorce."
> But I tell you that anyone who divorces his
> wife, except for marital unfaithfulness,
> causes her to become an adulteress, and
> anyone who marries the divorced woman
> commits adultery. (Matt. 5:31-32)

> I tell you that anyone who divorces his wife,
> except for marital unfaithfulness, and mar-
> ries another woman commits adultery.
> (Matt. 19:9)

In these two passages, Jesus challenges the views of
the two schools of Jewish thought (Shammai and Hillel).
He teaches that marriage is for life and should not be dis-
solved by divorce.

Defining the word *porneia* (translated "marital unfaithfulness") is a key element in trying to understanding these
passages. While some commentators teach that this word
refers to incestuous relationships or sexual promiscuity
during the betrothal period, most scholars believe the word
applies to relentless, persistent, and unrepentant adultery.
Among those holding to this exception clause for adultery,
some believe remarriage is possible while others do not.

The other significant section of teaching on divorce in
the New Testament can be found in Paul's instructions in
1 Corinthians 7:10–15.

> To the married I give this command (not I,
> but the Lord): A wife must not separate
> from her husband. But if she does, she must
> remain unmarried or else be reconciled to

her husband. And a husband must not divorce his wife.

To the rest I say this (I, not the Lord): If any brother has a wife who is not a believer and she is willing to live with him, he must not divorce her. And if a woman has a husband who is not a believer and he is willing to live with her, she must not divorce him. For the unbelieving husband has been sanctified through his wife, and the unbelieving wife has been sanctified through her believing husband. Otherwise your children would be unclean, but as it is, they are holy.

But if the unbeliever leaves, let him do so. A believing man or woman is not bound in such circumstances; God has called us to live in peace.

In the first section, Paul addresses Christians married to one another. Paul was obviously aware of the prevalence of divorce in the Greek world and of the legal right that a wife has to initiate a divorce. He gives the command for believers to stay married.

In the next section, Paul addresses the issue of mixed marriages. He says that in spite of religious incompatibility in such a marriage, the believing spouse is not to seek divorce. Some divorces may have been initiated because of the command of Ezra to the Israelites in Jerusalem after the Exile (Ezra 10:11) to divorce themselves from pagan spouses. Paul affirms the biblical principle: do not seek divorce. However, if the unbelieving spouse insists on divorce, the believer may have to yield to those proceedings and is not bound in such circumstances.

Based on the preceding verses, we can, therefore, conclude that a Christian can acquiesce to divorce in cases of marital infidelity by the other spouse or in cases of desertion by an unbelieving spouse. Yet even in these cases, the church should not encourage divorce. Certainly in very troubling cases that involve mental, sexual, and/or physical abuse, legal separation is available as a remedy to protect the abused spouse. God hates divorce; therefore Christians should never be in the position of encouraging or promoting divorce. Instead they should be encouraging reconciliation.

One final question: Is a divorced person eligible for a leadership position within the church? The key passage is 1 Timothy 3:2 which calls for a church leader to be above reproach and "the husband of but one wife." Rather than prohibiting a divorced person from serving in leadership, the language of this verse actually focuses on practicing polygamists. Polygamy was practiced in the first century and found among Jewish and Christian groups. The passage could be translated "a one-woman man." If Paul intended to prohibit a divorced person from leadership, he could have used a much less ambiguous term.

I believe, as Christians in a society where divorce is rampant, we must come back to these important biblical principles concerning marriage. Christians should work to build strong marriages. Pastors must frequently preach and teach about the importance of marriage. We should encourage fellow Christians to attend various marriage enrichment seminars and ministries in our community.

As Christians, I also believe we should reach out to those who have been through divorce. We must communicate Christ's forgiveness to them in the midst of their shattered lives. They need counseling and support groups. Often they also need financial help and direction as they begin to put together the shattered pieces of their lives.

But as we reach out to those whose lives are shattered by divorce, we must be careful that our ministry does not compromise our theology. We must reach out with both biblical convictions and biblical compassion. Marriage for life is God's ideal (Gen. 2), nevertheless, millions of people have been devastated by divorce and need to feel care and compassion from Christians. Churches have unfortunately erred on one side or another. Most churches have maintained a strong stand on marriage and divorce. While this strong biblical stand is admirable, it should also be balanced with compassion towards those caught in the throes of divorce. Strong convictions without compassionate outreach often seem to communicate that divorce is the unforgivable sin.

On the other hand, some churches in their desire to minister to divorced people have compromised their theological convictions. By starting out without biblically-based convictions about marriage and divorce, they have let their congregation's circumstances influence their theology.

Marriage for life is God's ideal, but divorce is a reality in our society. Christians should reach out with biblical convictions and biblical compassion to those affected by divorce. Christ's forgiveness can make an impact on the millions of lives shattered in the breaking of marriage covenants.

8

Adultery

Kerby Anderson

The seventh commandment says "You shall not commit adultery." Nevertheless, this sin has been committed throughout history. Today adultery seems more rampant than ever. While tabloid stories report the affairs of politicians, millionaires, and movie stars, films like *The English Patient, The Prince of Tides,* and *The Bridges of Madison County* feature and even promote adultery. Adultery seems to be practiced by everyone from a female B-52 bomber pilot to presidents.

How prevalent is adultery? The exact answer to that question is unclear. Accurate statistics on extramarital affairs are nearly impossible to establish because many people are unwilling to admit to an affair. Also, sociologists have found that some people may overstate their sexual behavior while others may understate their sexual behavior.

But, given those disclaimers, we can say that approximately two out of every three husbands commit adultery and one out of every two wives. The 1990 Kinsey Report suggests these numbers may be too high, but several marriage and family therapists judge the Kinsey numbers to be extremely conservative, if not totally inaccurate. Some other studies propose even higher numbers than the ones given above. For example, Sherry Hite argues in her controversial book that 70 percent of women married for more than five years are having sex outside their marriages, and 72 percent of men married more than two years are not monogamous.[1]

Whatever the actual numbers, the point to be made is that adultery is much more common than we would like to admit. Family therapist and psychiatrist Frank Pittman believes "there may be as many acts of infidelity in our society as there are traffic accidents."[2] He further argues that the fact that adultery has become commonplace has altered society's perception of it. He says, "We won't go back to the times when adulterers were put in the stocks and publicly humiliated or become one of those societies and there are many in which adultery is punishable by death. Society in any case is unable to enforce a rule that the majority of people break, and infidelity is so common it is no longer deviant."[3]

Perhaps you are thinking, "This is just a problem with non-Christians in society. It can't be a problem in the church. Certainly the moral standards of Christians are higher." Well, there is growing evidence that adultery is also a problem in Christian circles. An article in a 1997 issue of *Newsweek* magazine noted that various surveys suggest that as many as 30 percent of male Protestant ministers have had sexual relationships with women other than their wives.[4]

The *Journal of Pastoral Care,* in 1993, reported a survey of Southern Baptist pastors in which 14 percent acknowledged they had engaged in "sexual behavior inappropriate to a minister." It also reported that 70 percent had counseled at least one woman who had had intercourse with another minister.

A 1988 survey of nearly a thousand Protestant clergy by *Leadership* magazine found that 12 percent admitted to sexual intercourse outside of marriage, and 23 percent had done something sexually inappropriate with someone other than their spouse. The researchers also interviewed nearly a thousand subscribers to *Christianity Today* who were not pastors. They found the numbers were nearly double: 45 percent indicated having done something sexually inappropriate, and 23 percent admitted having extramarital intercourse.[5] Adultery is in society and is now in the church.

Myths About Adultery

Marital infidelity destroys marriages and families and often leads to divorce. Public sentiment against adultery is actually very strong. Approximately eight out of ten Americans disapprove of it.[6] Yet, even though most people consider adultery to be wrong and know that it can be devastating, our society still perpetuates a number of untruths about it through a popular mythology about extramarital affairs. At this point we want to examine some of the myths about adultery.

Myth 1: Adultery is about sex.

Often just the opposite seems the case. When a sexual affair is uncovered, observers often say, "What did he see in her?" or "What did she see in him?" Frequently the sex is better at home, and the marriage partner is at least as attractive as the adulterous partner.

Being pretty, handsome, or sensual is usually not the major issue. Partners in affairs are not usually chosen because they are prettier, more handsome, or sexier. They are chosen for various sorts of strange and nonsexual reasons. Usually the other woman or the other man in an adulterous relationship meets needs the spouse does not meet in the marriage. Dr. Willard Harley lists five primary needs for a man and five primary needs for a women in his book *His Needs, Her Needs: Building an Affair-Proof Marriage.*[7] He believes that unmet needs, by either partner, are a primary cause of extramarital affairs. He has also found that people wander into these affairs with astonishing regularity, in spite of whatever strong moral or religious convictions they may hold. A lack of fulfillment in one of these basic emotional areas creates a dangerous vacuum in a person's life. And, unfortunately, many will eventually fill that need outside of marriage.

Frank Pittman, author of the book *Private Lies: Infidelity and the Betrayal of Intimacy,* found in his own personal study that many of his patients who had affairs had a good sex life but came from marriages with little or no intimacy. He concluded, "Affairs were thus three times more likely to be the pursuit of a buddy than the pursuit of a better orgasm."[8]

Sex may not even be involved in some affairs. The relationship may be merely an emotional liaison. Counselor Bonnie Weil warns that these so-called "affairs of the heart can be even more treacherous than the purely physical kind. Women, particularly, are inclined to leave their husbands when they feel a strong emotional bond with another man."[9]

Myth 2: Adultery is about character.

In the past, society looked down on alcoholics as having weak characters because of their problem. Now we see alcoholism as an addiction or even as a disease. While that doesn't excuse the behavior, we can see that it can't be merely labeled as bad character. There is growing psychological evidence that adulterous behavior in parents dramatically affects children when they reach adulthood. Just as divorce in a family influences the likelihood of the adult children to consider divorce, adulterous behavior by parents seems to beget similar behavior by their offspring. Is this not one more example of the biblical teaching that the sins of one generation are visited upon the next?

Myth 3: Adultery is therapeutic.

Some of the psychology books and women's magazines circulating through our culture promote extramarital affairs. Depending on which source you are reading, an affair will make you a better lover, help you with your midlife crisis, bring joy into your life, or even bring excitement back into your marriage. Nothing could be further from the truth. An affair might give you more sex, but it could also give you a sexually transmitted disease. It might bring your marriage more excitement, if you consider a divorce court exciting. Remember that adultery results in divorce 65 percent of the time. "For most people and most marriages, infidelity is dangerous."[10]

Myth 4: Adultery is harmless.

Movies are just one venue in which adultery has been promoted positively. *The English Patient* received twelve Oscar nominations including Best Picture of the Year for its depiction of an adulterous relationship between a handsome count and the English-born wife of his colleague. *The Bridges of Madison County* relates the story of an Iowa farmer's wife who has a brief extramarital affair with a *National Geographic* photographer who supposedly helps re-energize her marriage. *The Prince of Tides* received seven Oscar nominations and shows a married therapist bedding down her also-married patient.

Notice the euphemisms that society has developed over the years to excuse or soften the perception of adultery. Many are not repeatable, but ones that are include: fooling around, sleeping around, flings, affairs, and dalliances. These and many other phrases perpetuate the notion that adultery is guilt-free and hurts no one. Some have even suggested that it's just a recreational activity like playing softball or going to the movies. Well, don't pass the popcorn, please.

Forbidden sex is an addiction that can—and usually does—have devastating consequences for an individual and a family. Adultery shatters trust, intimacy, and self-esteem. It breaks up families, ruins careers, and leaves a trail of pain and destruction in its wake. This potential legacy of emotional pain for one's children should be enough to make a person stop and count the cost before it's too late.

Even when affairs are never exposed, emotional costs are involved. For example, adulterous mates deprive their spouses of energy and intimacy that should go into the marriage. They deceive their marriage partners and become dishonest about their feelings and actions. As Frank Pittman says, "The infidelity is not in the sex, necessarily, but in the secrecy. It isn't whom you lie with. It's whom you lie to."[11]

Myth 5: Adultery has to end in divorce.

Only about 35 percent of couples remain together after the discovery of an adulterous affair; the other 65 percent divorce. Perhaps nothing can destroy a marriage faster than marital infidelity.

The good news is that it doesn't have to be that way. One counselor claims that 98 percent of the couples she treats remain together after counseling. Granted, this success rate is not easy to achieve and requires immediate moral choices and forgiveness. It does demonstrate, however, that adultery need not end in divorce.

How can a couple prevent adultery? Dr. Willard Harley, in his book *His Needs, Her Needs,* provides some answers. He has found that marriages that fail to meet a spouse's needs are more vulnerable to an extramarital affair. Often, the failure of men and women to meet each other's needs is due to a lack of knowledge rather than a selfish unwillingness to be considerate. Meeting these needs is critically important because in marriages that fail to meet needs, it is striking and alarming how consistently people seek to satisfy these unmet needs through an extramarital affair. If any of a spouse's five basic needs goes unmet, that spouse becomes vulnerable to the temptation of an affair.

Preventing Adultery: Her Needs

First, let's look at the five needs of a wife.

Affection

The first need is for affection. To most women affection symbolizes security, protection, comfort, and approval. When a husband shows his wife affection, he sends the following messages: (1) I'll take care of you and protect you; (2) I'm concerned about the problems you face, and I am with you; (3) I think you've done a good job, and I'm proud of you.

Men need to understand how strongly women need these affirmations. For the typical wife, there can hardly be enough of them. A hug can communicate all of the affirmations of the previous paragraph. But, affection can be shown in many other ways: kisses, cards, flowers, dinners out, opening the car door, holding hands, walks after dinner, back rubs, phone calls—there are a thousand ways to say "I love you." From a woman's point of view, affection is the essential cement of her relationship with a man.

Conversation

The second need is conversation. Wives need their husbands to talk to them and listen to them; they need lots of two-way conversation. In their dating life prior to marriage, most couples spent time showing each other affection and talking. This shouldn't be dropped after the wedding. When two people get married, each partner has a right to expect the same loving care and attention that prevailed during courtship. The man who takes time to talk to a woman will have an inside track to her heart.

Honesty and Openness

The third need is honesty and openness. A wife needs to trust her husband totally. A sense of security is the common thread woven through all of a woman's five basic needs. If a husband does not keep up honest and open communication with his wife, he undermines her trust and eventually destroys her security. To feel secure, a wife must trust her husband to give her accurate information about his past, the present, and the future. If she can't trust the signals he sends, she has no foundation on which to build a solid relationship. Instead of adjusting to him, she always feels off balance; instead of growing toward him, she grows away from him.

Financial Commitment

Financial commitment is a fourth need a wife experiences. She needs enough money to live comfortably; she needs financial support. No matter how successful a career a woman might have, she usually wants her husband to earn enough money to allow her to feel supported and cared for.

Family Commitment

The fifth need is family commitment. A wife needs her husband to be a good father and to be committed to his family. The vast majority of women who get married have a powerful instinct to create a home and have children. Above all, wives want their husbands to take a leadership role in the family and to dedicate themselves to the moral and educational development of their children.

Preventing Adultery: His Needs

Now, let's look at the five needs husbands have.

Sexual Fulfillment

The first is sexual fulfillment. The typical wife doesn't understand her husband's deep need for sex any more than the typical husband understands his wife's deep need for affection. But these two ingredients can work very closely together in a happy, fulfilled marriage. Sex can come naturally and often, if there is enough affection.

Recreational Companionship

The second need for a man is recreational companionship. He needs her to be his playmate. It is not uncommon for women, when they are single, to join men in pursuing their interests. They find themselves hunting, fishing, playing outdoor games, and watching sports and movies they would never have chosen on their own.

After marriage, wives often try to interest their husbands in activities more to their own liking. If their attempts fail, they may encourage their husbands to continue their recreational activities without them. But this option is very dangerous to a marriage, because men place surprising importance on having their wives as recreational companions. Among the five basic male needs, spending recreational time with his wife is second only to sex for the typical husband.

An Attractive Spouse

A husband's third need is an attractive spouse. A man needs a wife who looks good to him. Dr. Harley states that in sexual relationships, most men find it nearly impossible to appreciate a woman for her inner qualities alone—there must be more. A man's need for physical attractiveness in a mate is profound.

Domestic Support

The fourth need for a man is domestic support. He needs peace and quiet. So deep is a husband's need for domestic support from his wife that he often fantasizes about how she will greet him lovingly and pleasantly at the door, about well-behaved children who likewise act glad to see him and welcome him to the comfort of a well-maintained home.

The fantasy continues as his wife urges him to sit down and relax before taking part in a tasty dinner. Later, the family goes out for an evening stroll, and he returns to put the children to bed with no hassle or fuss. Then he and his wife relax, talk together, and perhaps watch a little television until they retire at a reasonable hour to love each other. Wives may chuckle at this scenario, but this vision is quite common in the fantasy lives of many men. The male need for his wife to "take care of things"—especially him—is widespread, persistent, and deep.

Admiration

The fifth need is admiration. He needs her to be proud of him. Wives need to learn how to express the admiration they already feel for their husbands instead of pressuring them to greater achievements. Honest admiration is a great motivator for men. When a woman tells a man she thinks he's wonderful, that inspires him to achieve more. He sees himself capable of handling new responsibilities and perfecting skills far above those of his present level.

If any of a spouse's five basic needs go unmet, that person becomes vulnerable to the temptation of an affair. Therefore, the best way to prevent adultery is to meet the needs of your spouse and make your marriage strong.

Feminist Myths
Kerby Anderson

A s someone who works in the media, I am well aware that once certain myths get started they have a life of their own. A number of these myths are promoted and disseminated by feminists and can be found in the book *Who Stole Feminism?*[1] The author, Christina Hoff Sommers, though a feminist, has been concerned for some time about the prominence of these myths and does a masterful job tracing down the origin of each and setting the record straight. If you want more information on any of them, I would recommend you obtain her well-documented book.

The Extent of Anorexia Nervosa

In her book *Revolution from Within,* Gloria Steinem informed her readers that "in this country alone . . . about 150,000 females die of anorexia each year."[2] To put this dramatic statistic in perspective, the number is more than three times the annual number of fatalities from car accidents for the total population. The only problem with the statistic is that it is absolutely false.

Lest you think that this was a mere typographical error, consider the following. The statistic also appears in the feminist best-seller *The Beauty Myth* by Naomi Wolf.

"How," she asks, "would America react to the mass self-immolation by hunger of its favorite sons?" While admitting that "nothing justifies comparison with the Holocaust," she nevertheless makes just such a comparison. "When confronted with a vast number of emaciated bodies starved not by nature but by men, one must notice a certain resemblance."[3]

What was the source of this statistic? Ms. Wolf got her figures from *Fasting Girls: The Emergence of Anorexia Nervosa as a Modern Disease* by Joan Brumberg, a historian and former director of women's studies at Cornell University.[4] It turns out that she misquoted the American Anorexia and Bulimia Association which had stated that there are 150,000 to 200,000 sufferers (not fatalities) of anorexia nervosa. The actual figure is many orders of magnitude lower. According to the National Center for Health Statistics, there were seventy deaths from anorexia in 1990. Even seventy deaths is tragic, but seventy deaths out of a population of over 100 million women can hardly be considered a holocaust.

Apparently Naomi Wolf plans to revise her numbers in an updated version of *The Beauty Myth,* but the figure is now widely accepted as true. Ann Landers repeated it in her 1992 column by stating that "every year, 150,000 American women die from complications associated with anorexia and bulimia." The false statistic has also made it into college textbooks. A women's studies text, aptly titled *The Knowledge Explosion,* contains the erroneous figure in its preface.

The Incidence of Domestic Violence

In November 1992, Deborah Louis, president of the National Women's Studies Association, sent a message to the Women's Studies Electronic Bulletin Board. It read, "According to [the] last March of Dimes report, domestic violence (vs. pregnant women) is now responsible for more birth defects than all other causes combined."[5] On February 23, 1993, Patricia Ireland, president of the National Organization for Women, said on the Charlie Rose program that "battery of pregnant women is the number one cause of birth defects in this country."

Certainly unsettling data. But again, the biggest problem is that the statistic is absolutely false. The March of Dimes never published the study and did not know of any research that corroborated the statement.

Nevertheless, journalists willingly recited the erroneous statistic. The *Boston Globe* reported that "domestic violence is the leading cause of birth defects, more than all other medical causes combined, according to a March of Dimes study." The *Dallas Morning News* reported that "the March of Dimes has concluded that the battering of women during pregnancy causes more birth defects than all the diseases put together for which children are usually immunized."

When *Time* magazine published essentially the same article, the rumor started spinning out of control.[6] Concerned citizens and legislators called the March of Dimes for the study. Eventually the error was traced to Sarah Buel, a founder of the domestic violence advocacy project at Harvard Law School. She had misunderstood a statement made by a nurse who noted that a March of Dimes study showed that more women are screened for birth defects than they are for domestic battery. The nurse had never said anything about battery causing birth defects.

Although we could merely chalk this error up to a misunderstanding, it is disturbing that so many newspapers and magazines reported it uncritically. Battery causing birth defects? More than genetic disorders like spina bifida, Downs syndrome, Tay-Sachs disease, sickle-cell anemia? More than alcohol, crack, or AIDS? Where was the press in checking the facts? Why are feminist myths so easily repeated in the press?

Increased Violence on Super Bowl Sunday

In January 1993, newspaper and television networks reported an alarming statistic. They stated that the incidence of domestic violence tended to rise by 40 percent on Super Bowl Sunday. NBC, which was broadcasting the game, made a special plea for men to stay calm. Feminists called for emergency preparations in anticipation of the expected increase in violence.

Feminists also used the occasion to link masculinity and violence against women. Nancy Isaac, a Harvard School of Public Health research associate specializing in domestic violence, told the *Boston Globe,* "It's a day for men to revel in their maleness and, unfortunately, for a lot of men that includes being violent toward women if they want to be."[7]

Nearly every journalist accepted the 40 percent figure—except for Ken Ringle at the *Washington Post.* He checked the facts and was able to expose the myth, but not before millions of Americans were indoctrinated with the feminist myth of male aggression during Super Bowl Sunday.

The Incidence of Rape Against Women

The Justice Department says that 8 percent of all American women will be victims of rape or attempted rape in their lifetime. Feminist legal scholar Catherine MacKinnon, however, claims that rape happens to almost half of all women at least once in their lives.[8] Who is right? Obviously, the difference between these two statistics stems from a number of factors ranging from underreporting rape to very different definitions of what constitutes rape.

The Justice Department figure is obviously low since it is based on the number of cases reported to the police, and rape is the most underreported of crimes. The feminist figures are artificially high because they use broad definitions of rape and let the questioner rather than the victim decide whether there was a rape or not. The two most frequently cited studies are the 1985 *Ms.* magazine study and the 1992 National Women's Study. The *Ms.* magazine study of three thousand college students gave a statistic of about one in four for women who have been raped or were victims of an attempted rape. However, the study's broad definition of rape sometimes included kissing, fondling, and other activities that few people would call rape. In fact, only 27 percent of those women counted as having been raped actually labeled themselves as rape victims. Also, 42 percent of those counted as rape victims went on to have sex with their "attackers" on a later occasion.

The National Women's Study released a figure stating that one in eight women have been raped. Again, the surveyors used extremely broad, expanded definitions of rape that allowed the surveyor to decide if a woman had been raped or not.

The statistics for "date rape" and rape on campus have also been exaggerated. Camille Paglia warns that "date rape has swelled into a catastrophic cosmic event, like an asteroid threatening the earth in a fifties science-fiction film."[9] Added to this is the date-rape hype on most college campuses that includes rallies, marches, and date-rape counseling groups.

Peter Hellman, writing for *New York* magazine on the subject of rape on campus, was surprised to find that campus police logs at Columbia University showed no evidence of rape on campus. Only two rapes were reported to the Columbia campus police, and in both cases, the charges were dropped for lack of evidence.[10] Hellman checked figures for other campuses and found a rate of less than 0.5 rape to a campus. He also found that public monies were being spent disproportionately on campus rape programs while community rape programs were scrambling for dollars.

The high rape numbers serve feminists by promoting the belief that American culture is sexist and misogynist. They also help liberal politicians by providing justification for additional funding for social services. Senator Joseph Biden introduced the Violence Against Women Act to "raise the consciousness of the American public." He argued that violence against women is much like racial violence and calls for civil as well as criminal remedies.

Female Self-Esteem

In 1991, newspapers around the country proclaimed that the self-esteem of teenage girls was falling. The *New York Times* announced, "Little girls lose their self-esteem on the way to adolescence, study finds."[11]

The study was commissioned by the American Association of University Women (AAUW) to measure the self-esteem of girls and boys between the ages of nine and fifteen. The poll seemed to show that between the ages of eleven and sixteen, girls experience a dramatic drop in self-esteem, which, in turn, significantly affects their ability to learn and to achieve. The report made headlines around the country and led to hundreds of conferences and community action projects.

Here is how the AAUW summarized the results of the survey in their brochure: "In a crucial measure of self-esteem, 60 percent of elementary school girls and 69 percent of elementary school boys say they are 'happy the way I am.' But, by high school, girls' self-esteem falls 31 percent to only 29 percent, while boys' self-esteem falls only 23 percent to 46 percent."[12]

Girls are less likely than boys to say they are "pretty good at a lot of things." Less than a third of girls express this confidence, compared to almost half the boys. A 10-percentage-point gender gap in confidence in their abilities increases to 19 percentage points in high school.

It turns out that the report didn't even define the term *self-esteem,* or promote an informal discussion of what the authors meant by it. Other researchers suspect that the apparent gap in self-esteem may merely reflect a gap in expressiveness. Girls and women are more aware of their feelings and more articulate in expressing them, and so they are more candid about their negative emotions in self-reports than boys and men are.

When asked how often they are "good at a lot of things," boys more often answered, "All the time," whereas girls, being more reflective, gave more nuanced answers ("some of the time" or "usually"). Although the surveyors decided that the girls' response showed poor self-esteem, it may merely reflect a "maturity gap" between boys and girls. Boys, lacking maturity, reflectiveness, and humility, are more likely to answer the question as "always true."

Discrimination Against Girls in School

An American Association of University Women (AAUW) report argued that schools and teachers were biased against girls in the classroom.[13] The *Wellesley Report,* published in 1992, argued that there was a gender bias in education. The *Boston Globe* proclaimed that "from the very first days in school, American girls face a drum-fire of gender bias, ranging from sexual harassment to discrimination in the curriculum to lack of attention from teachers, according to a survey released today in Washington."[14] The release of this study was again followed by great media attention and the convening of conferences. It also provided the intellectual ammunition for the Gender Equity in Education bill introduced in 1993 by Patricia Schroeder, Susan Molinari, and others. It would have established a permanent and well-funded gender equity bureaucracy.

Are women really being damaged by our school system? Today 55 percent of college students are female, and women receive 52 percent of the bachelor's degrees. Yes, girls seem somewhat behind in math and science, but those math and science test differentials are small compared with the large differentials favoring girls in reading and writing.

The study also assumed that teachers' verbal interactions with students indicated how much they valued them. The surveyors therefore deduced that teachers valued boys more than girls. However, teachers often give more attention to boys because they are more immature and require the teacher to keep them in line. Most girls, being more mature, don't want the attention or verbal discipline and need less negative attention to get their work done.

The Gender Wage Gap

A major rallying cry during the debates on comparable worth was that women make fifty-nine cents for every dollar men do. The figure is now seventy-one cents. But if you factor in age, length of time in the workplace, and type of job, the wage gap is much smaller for younger women. Those with children tend to make slightly less than those without children, but it's closer to ninety cents.

Feminists argue that the pay gap is a vivid illustration of discrimination. Economists argue that it's due to shorter workweeks and less workplace experience. It is, no doubt, also due to the kind of jobs women choose. Women generally prefer clean, safe places with predictable hours and less stress. The more dangerous, dirty, and high-pressure jobs generally appeal to men, which is reflected in salary differences.

Lots of myths circulate through society, especially through the Western media. The next time you hear or read one of these myths (or others like them) check out the facts.

10

Ten Lies of Feminism

Sue Bohlin

This chapter examines the ten lies of feminism that Dr. Toni Grant suggests in her book *Being a Woman.*[1]

> At its inception, the feminist movement, accompanied by the sexual revolution, made a series of enticing, exciting promises to women. These promises sounded good, so good that many women deserted their men and their children or rejected the entire notion of marriage and family, in pursuit of "themselves" and a career. These pursuits, which emphasized self-sufficiency and individualism, were supposed to enhance a woman's quality of life and improve her options, as well as her relations with men. Now, a decade or so later, women have had to face the fact that, in many ways, feminism and liberation made promises that could not be delivered.[2]

Lie 1: Women can have it all.

The first lie is that women can have it all. We are fed an illusion that women, the superior sex, have inexhaustible physical and emotional energy to juggle a career, family, friendships, and volunteer service. Proponents of feminism have declared that, not only *can* women do what men do; we *ought to do* what men do. Since men can't do what women can do—have babies—this put a double burden on women. It wasn't enough that women were already exhausted from the never-ending tasks of child-rearing and homemaking; we were told that women needed to be in the workforce as well, contributing to the family financially.

Scripture presents a different picture for men and women. The Bible appears to make a distinction between each gender's primary energies. The commands to women are generally in the realm of our relationships, which is consistent with the way God made women. They are primarily relational, naturally sensitive to others, and usually valuing people above things. Scripture never forbids women to be gainfully employed; in fact, the virtuous woman of Proverbs 31 is engaged in several part-time business ventures, in real estate and manufacturing. Nonetheless, it is the excellent care of her husband, her children, her home, and her community that inspires the praise she is due. Titus 2 instructs older women to mentor younger women, and teach them to care for their husbands and children and homemaking responsibilities.

The God-given strengths of a woman were given to bring glory to God through her womanly differences.

Lie 2: Men and women are fundamentally the same.

Apart from some minor biological differences, feminism strongly suggested that males and females are fundamentally the same. Culture turns blank human slates into truck-wielding boys and doll-toting girls. This lie has been very effective in changing our culture.

My husband Ray and I offer a seminar at Probe's Mind Games conferences called "Guys Are from Mars, Girls Are from Venus," where we go over the major differences between the sexes. Men, for instance, tend to be more goal-oriented and competitive, where women are more relational and cooperative. Men are active; women are verbal. This is intuitively obvious to the adults in our audience, but it is often news to high school and college students. We find adults nodding with smiles of recognition, some of them nudging each other in the ribs.

In the younger members of the audience, though, we see "the lights come on" in their eyes as they are exposed to something that is obvious and that they probably already knew was true. Feminism's worldview has been feeding them a lie. They have been so immersed in this cultural myth that they have accepted it without question.

One young man came up to me after a session and said he totally disagreed with me, that there are no real differences between males and females. I asked him if he treated his guy friends the same way he treated his girl friends, and he said, "Of course!" I asked, "And this doesn't cause you any problems?" He said no.

With a smile, I suggested he come talk to me in ten years, after he'd had a chance to experience real life!

The truth is that God created significant differences between males and females. We can see evidence of this in the fact that Scripture gives different commands for husbands and wives, which are rooted in the differing needs and divinely appointed roles of men and women.

Lie 3: Desirability is enhanced by achievement.

The third lie of feminism is that the more a woman achieves, the more attractive and desirable she becomes to men. The importance of achievement to a man's sense of self—an element of masculinity that is, we believe, God-given —has been projected onto women. Feminism declared that achieving something, making a mark in the world, was the only measure of success that merited the respect of others. Women who believed this myth found themselves competing with men. Now, competition is appropriate in the business and professional world, but it's disastrous in relationships.

Men do respect and admire accomplished women, just as they do men, but personal relationships operate under a different set of standards. Men most appreciate a woman's unique feminine attributes: love, sensitivity, her ability to relate. Women have been shocked to discover that their hard-won accomplishments haven't resulted in great relationships with men. Sometimes being overeducated hampers a woman's ability to relate to men. Men's egos are notoriously fragile, and they are by nature competitive. It's threatening to many men when a woman achieves more, or accomplishes more, or knows more than they do. Feminism didn't warn women of the double standard in relationships—that achievement can and does reap benefits in our careers, but can be a stumbling block in our relationships.

The question naturally arises, then: Is it bad for a woman to have a higher degree of education than the man in a relationship? Is it troublesome when a woman is smarter than the man? Should a woman "dumb down" in order to get or keep her man?

In the words of the apostle Paul, "May it never be!" A

woman living up to the potential of her God-given gifts brings glory to God; it would be an insult to our gracious God to pretend those gifts aren't there. The answer is for women to understand that many men feel threatened and insecure about this area of potential competition, and for them to maintain an attitude of humility and sensitivity about their strengths; as Romans exhorts us, "Honor[ing] one another above yourselves" (12:10).

Not surprisingly, God already knows about the disparity between the sexes on the issue of achievement. Throughout the Bible, men are called to trust God as they achieve whatever God has called them to do. It's important for men to experience personal significance by making their mark in the world. But God calls women to trust Him in a different area—in their relationships. A woman's value is usually not in providing history-changing leadership and making great, bold moves, but in loving and supporting those around them, changing the world by touching hearts. Once in a while a woman does read a high level of achievement on a national or global scale; consider the biblical judge Deborah, Golda Meir, Margaret Thatcher, and Indira Gandhi. But women like these are the exception, not the rule. And we don't have to feel guilty for not being "exceptional."

Lie 4: We must reach our "unrealized potential."

Lie number four says that all of us—but especially women—have tremendous potential that simply must be realized. To feminism's way of thinking, just being average isn't acceptable; you must be great.

This causes two problems. First, women are deceived into thinking they are of the elite, the few, the special.

Reality, though, is that most women are ordinary, one of the many. All of us are uniquely gifted by God, but few women are given visible, high-profile leadership roles, which tend to be the only ones that feminism deems valuable. We run into trouble when we're operating under a set of beliefs that don't coincide with reality!

Consequently, many women are operating under unrealistically high expectations of themselves. When life doesn't deliver on their hopes, whether they want to be class valedictorians, beauty pageant winners, company presidents, or neurosurgeons, women are set up for major disappointment. Just being a cog in the wheel of your own small world isn't enough.

This brings us to the second problem. A lot of women beat themselves up for not accomplishing greatness. Instead of investing their life's energies in doing well those things they can do, they grieve over what and who they are not. Just being good, or being good at what they do, isn't enough if they're not the best.

Romans 12:3 tells us, "Do not think of yourself more highly than you ought." Rather than worrying about our unrealized potential for some sort of nebulous greatness, we should be concerned about being faithful and obedient in the things God has given us to do, trusting Him for the ultimate results. And we should not worry about being ordinary as if there were some stigma to it. Scripture says that God is pleased to use ordinary people, because that's how He gets the most glory (see 1 Cor. 1:26–31). There is honor in being an ordinary person in the hand of an extraordinary God.

Lie 5: Men and women have the same sexual
    needs.

The fifth lie of feminism is that men and women are the same sexually. This lie comes to us courtesy of the same evil source that brought us the lies of the sexual revolution.

The truth is that women can't separate sex from love as easily as men can. For women, sex needs to be an expression of love and commitment. Without these qualities, sex is demeaning—nothing more than hormones going crazy.

The cost of sex is far greater for women than for men. Sex outside of a committed, loving relationship—I'm talking about marriage here—often results in unplanned pregnancy, sexually transmitted diseases, and profound heartbreak. Every time a woman gives her body away to a man, she gives a part of her heart as well. Sexual "freedom" has brought new degrees of heartache to millions of women. The lie of sexual equality has produced widespread promiscuity and epidemic disease. No wonder so many women are struggling with self-esteem!

God's commands concerning sex take into account the fact that men and women are not the same sexually or any other way. He tells us to exercise self-control before marriage, saving all sexual expression for the constraints of a marriage relationship, and then to keep the marriage bed pure once we are married. When we follow these guidelines, we discover that God's laws provide protection for women: the security of a committed relationship, freedom from sexual health worries, and a stable environment for any children produced in the union. This high standard also protects men by providing a safe channel for their sexual energies. Both chaste single men, and faithful husbands, are kept safe from sexual diseases, unwanted pregnancies with women other than their wives, and the guilt of sexual sin.

Lie 6: Maternity should be delayed until after other achievements.

Many women have postponed marriage and childbearing to pursue their own personal development and career goals. This perspective denies the reality of a woman's reproductive system and the limitations of time. Childbearing is easier in a woman's twenties and thirties than in her forties. Plus, there is a physical cost; science has shown the liabilities that older women incur for themselves and their babies. Midlife women are more apt to have problems getting pregnant and staying pregnant, and they often experience difficult deliveries. The risk of conceiving a child with Down's syndrome is considerably higher in older mothers.[3] In addition, fertility treatment doesn't work as well for women over forty.[4]

There is also a spiritual dimension to denying maternity. When women refuse their God-ordained roles and responsibilities, they open themselves to spiritual deception and temptations. Intriguing is 1 Timothy 2:15: "But women will be saved through childbearing." In one compelling translation, "Women will be kept safe through childbearing," Paul uses the word for childbearing as a sort of shorthand for the woman's involvement in the domestic sphere—having her "focus on the family," so to speak.[5] When a married woman's priorities are marriage, family, and the home, she is kept safe—protected—from the consequences of delaying motherhood and the temptations that beleaguer a woman trying to fill a man's role. For example, I know one married woman who chose to pursue a full-time career in commercial real estate, to the detriment of her family. She confessed that she found herself constantly battling the temptation to lust on two fronts: sexual lust for the men in her office and her clients, and lust for the recognition and material things that marked success in that field. Another friend chose her career over having any children at all, and discovered that, like the men in her field, she could not separate her sense of self from her job, and it ultimately cost her her marriage and her life as she knew it. The problem isn't having a career; the problem is getting our priorities out of balance.

Lie 7: To be "feminine" is to be weak.

In the attempt to blur gender distinctions, feminists declared war on the concept of gender-related characteristics. The qualities that marked feminine women—softness, sweetness, kindness, the ability to relate well—were judged as silly, stupid, and weak. Only what characterized men—traits like firmness, aggressiveness, competitiveness—were deemed valuable.

But when women try to take on male qualities, the end result is a distortion that is neither feminine nor masculine. A woman is perceived as shrill, not spirited. What is acceptable aggression in a man is perceived as unwelcome brashness in a woman. When women try to be tough, it is often taken as unpleasantness. Unfortunately, there really is a strong stereotype about "what women should be like" that merits being torn down. A lot of men are threatened by strong women with opinions and agendas of their own and treat them with undeserved disrespect. But it is not true that traditionally masculine characteristics are the only ones that count.

There really is a double standard operating, because the characteristics that constitute masculinity and femininity are separate and different, and they are not interchangeable.

To be feminine is a special kind of strength. It's a different, appealing kind of power that allows a woman to influence the world in a way quite distinct from the way a man influences the world. It pleased the Lord to create woman to complement man, not to compete with him or be a more rounded copy of him. According to 1 Corinthians 11:7, man is the image and glory of God, but woman is the glory of man. Femininity isn't weakness; it's the glorious, splendid crown on humanity.

Lie 8: Doing is better than being.

In his book *Men Are from Mars, Women Are from Venus,*[6] John Gray points out that men get their sense of self from achievement, and women get their sense of self from relationships. Feminism declared that the male orientation of what you do was the only one that mattered. Who you were, and how important you were to the people in your world, didn't count for as much.

This lie said that active is good, passive is bad. Traditional feminine behaviors of being passive and receptive were denounced as demeaning to women and ineffective in the world. Only being the initiator counted, not being the responder. "To listen, to be there, to receive the other with an open heart and mind—this has always been one of the most vital roles of woman. Most women do this quite naturally, but many have come to feel uneasy in this role. Instead, they work frantically on assertiveness, aggression, personal expression, and power, madly suppressing their feminine instincts of love and relatedness."[7]

Women's roles in the family, the church, and the world are a combination of being a responder and an initiator. As a responder, a wife honors her husband through loving submission, and a woman serves the church through the exercise of her spiritual gifts. As an initiator and leader, a woman teaches her children and uses her abilities in the world, as did the woman of Proverbs 31. God's plan is for us to live a balanced life—sometimes active, sometimes passive; sometimes the initiator, sometimes the responder; at all times, submitting both who we are and what we do to the lordship of Christ.

Lie 9: Women are totally self-sufficient.

The ninth lie is the myth of self-sufficiency. Remember the famous feminist slogan that appeared on everything from bumper stickers to T-shirts to notepads? "A woman without a man is like a fish without a bicycle." The message was clear: Women don't need men, who are inferior anyway. The world would be a better place if women ran it: no wars, no greed, no power plays, just glorious cooperation and peace.

The next step after "women don't need men" was logical: Women don't need anybody. We can take care of ourselves. Helen Reddy's hit song "I Am Woman" became feminism's theme song, with the memorable chorus, "If I have to, I can do anything / I am strong / I am invincible / I am woman!"

Of course, if women don't need anybody except themselves, they certainly don't need God. Particularly a masculine, patriarchal God who makes rules they don't like and insists that He alone is God. But the need to worship is deeply ingrained in us, so feminist thought gave rise to goddess worship. The goddess was just a female image to focus on; in actuality, goddess worship is worship of oneself.[8]

The lie of self-sufficiency is the same lie that Satan has been deceiving us with since the Garden of Eden: What do you need God for? We grieve the Lord's heart when we believe this lie. Jeremiah 2:13 says, "My people have committed two sins: They have forsaken me, the spring of living water, and have dug their own cisterns, broken cisterns that cannot hold water." God made us for Himself; believing the lie of self-sufficiency isn't only futile, it's a slap in God's face.

Lie 10: Women would enjoy the feminization of men.

The tenth lie of feminism is that women would enjoy the feminization of men. Feminists believed that the only way to achieve equality of the sexes was to do away with role distinctions. Then they decided that that wasn't enough. Society had to do away with gender distinctions, or at the very least blur the lines. Women embraced more masculine values, and men were encouraged to embrace more feminine characteristics. That was supposed to fix the problem. It didn't.

As men tried to be "good guys" and accommodate feminists' demands, the culture saw a new type of man emerge: sensitive, nurturing, warmly compassionate, yielding. The only problem was that this "soft man" wasn't what women wanted. Women pushed men to be like women, and when they complied, nobody respected them. Women, it turns out, want to be the soft ones—and we want men to be strong and firm and courageous; we want a manly man. When men start taking on feminine characteristics, they're just wimpy and unmasculine. They're not pleasing themselves or the women who demanded the change. There is a good reason that books and movies with strong, masculine heroes continue to appeal to such a large audience. Both men and women respond to men who fulfill God's design for male leadership, protectiveness, and strength.

Underlying the women's liberation movement is an angry, unsubmissive attitude that is fueled by lies. It's good to know what the lies are, but it's also important to know what God's Word says, so we can combat them with the power of His truth.

11

Why Dr. Laura Is (Usually) Right

Sue Bohlin

Dr. Laura Schlessinger's call-in radio show has the second largest audience in the country behind Rush Limbaugh. She describes it as a "no-nonsense, in-your-face, responsibility-driven talk show." Her refusal to coddle people's self-centered behavior and immoral or stupid choices is either highly entertaining or absolutely infuriating, depending on your worldview. She's opinionated and not afraid to fly in the face of the culture. Most of the time I agree with her, but sometimes she misses the boat. In this chapter I'll be looking at why Dr. Laura is usually right—not because her positions are agreeable, but because they are consistent with what God has revealed in the Bible.

Dr. Laura rejects the victim mentality. She says, "Victimization status is the modern promised land of absolution from personal responsibility. Nobody is acknowledged to have free will or responsibility anymore."[1] Instead of coddling people because of difficult past experiences, she calls her audience to make right choices. In her book *How Could You Do That?* she writes, "I don't believe for a minute that everything that happens to you is your doing or your fault. But I do believe the ultimate quality of your life, and your happiness, is determined by your courageous and ethical choices, and your overall attitude."[2] This call to assume responsibility for our choices and our behaviors resonates with us because it is consistent with the dignity God betowed on us when He gave us the ability to make significant choices and not be His puppets. Joshua encouraged the Israelites, "Choose for yourselves this day whom you will serve. . . . But as for me and my household, we will serve the LORD" (Josh. 24:15). It was a real choice with real consequences. That's because we live in a cause-and-effect universe where "God cannot be mocked. A man reaps what he sows"(Gal. 6:7).

Dr. Laura includes a most interesting postscript in her book *How Could You Do That?* She quotes from the Genesis 4 passage where God confronts Cain for his bad attitude after He would not accept Cain's offering. God tells Cain, "If you do what is right, will you not be accepted? But if you do not do what is right, sin is crouching at your door; it desires to have you, but you must master it" (Gen. 4:7). She makes the point that God seems to be teaching that there is joy in doing right, and "God also reassures us that we do have the capacity to rise above circumstance and attain mastery over our weaker selves."[3] It's a good observation, and this passage makes a strong statement about what God expects of every person, as a moral creature made in His image. He wants us to do what is right and resist the pull of sin's temptation. Much of Dr. Laura's "preaching, teaching and nagging" (her words) is directed at helping people decide to make good moral choices. Even if they don't know God, their lives will work better simply because they will be more in line with how God created us to live.

Dr. Laura's emphasis on honor, integrity, and ethics strikes a nerve in 20 million listeners.[4] No surprise, really: that nerve is common to all of us—the nerve called morality —because we are made in the image of a moral God.

Self-Esteem

Dr. Laura's values and beliefs attract millions of listeners to her daily radio program. One reason is her common-sense approach to the whole issue of self-esteem. When a caller complains, "I don't feel very good about myself," Dr. Laura will fire back a great question: "Why *should* you feel good about yourself? What have you done that gives you a reason to feel good about yourself?" In a culture where people want to believe they're wonderful and worthwhile without any basis for such an assessment, Dr. Laura has a completely different approach: self-esteem is earned.

Ways to Earn Self-Respect

In her books and on her radio show, she suggests several means of earning the right to enjoy self-respect, and all of them are good ideas from a pragmatic perspective.

Dr. Laura points out that we derive pleasure from having character. We need to choose high moral values and then honor them during times of temptation. She writes, "There is no fast lane to self-esteem. It's won on . . . battlegrounds where immediate gratification comes up against character. When character triumphs, self-esteem heightens."[5]

She also says that choosing personal and professional integrity over moral compromise will make us feel good about ourselves in the long run. So will valuing and honoring our responsibilities, which she calls "the express route" to self-esteem.[6] We build self-respect by choosing loyalty, sacrifice, and self-reliance over short-term self-indulgence.[7]

In her book *Ten Stupid Things Women Do to Mess Up Their Lives,* Dr. Laura astutely demonstrates one of the differences between the sexes: "Women tend to make a relationship their life, their identity, while men make it a part of their lives."[8] She's absolutely right. The reason a relationship cannot provide true self-esteem for a woman is the same reason a man's job or accomplishments can't do it. It is idolatry to look to relationships or accomplishments for meaning and purpose. God will never honor our false gods.

But self-esteem is only part of the equation for a healthy view of ourselves. Self-esteem is how we feel about ourselves; it needs to be built on the foundation of how we think about ourselves, which is our sense of self-worth. How valuable am I? What makes me significant? It doesn't matter how good we feel about ourselves if we're, in actuality, worthless.

Pastor Don Matzat tells of a woman who came to him complaining, "I feel like I am completely worthless." He blew her away with his response. Gently and slowly, he said, "Maybe you are completely worthless."[9] Are you shocked? This lady was. But he's right. We are only valuable because God made us, not because of anything within ourselves. We are infinitely precious because He made us in His image. God can dwell in us. And He proved our value by paying an unimaginable price for us: the lifeblood of His very Son. Apart from God, we are completely worthless.

If we are only valuable because God made us in His image, why did He give His Son for us? C. S. Lewis put it so well: "Christ did not die for men because they were intrinsically worth dying for, but because He is intrinsically love, and therefore loves infinitely."[10]

Dr. Laura's right; we earn our self-respect. But our sense of worth is one of God's great gifts to us, because it is His love that determines our value.

Human Beings as Moral Creatures

If you call Dr. Laura's radio program, the screener will ask, "What is your moral dilemma? What is the issue of right and wrong that you want to discuss?" Zeroing in on moral problems and not psychological ones sets her call-in talk show apart from most others. Dr. Laura sees human beings as moral creatures, capable of choosing good and evil.

Why do people do good things? This is what she wrote in her book, *How Could You Do That?:* "In contrast to all other creatures on earth, only humans measure themselves against ideals of motivation and action. We are elevated above all other creatures because we have a moral sense: a notion of right and wrong and a determination to bring significance to our lives beyond mere existence and survival, by actions that are selfless and generous."[11]

It's true, we are indeed elevated above all other creatures by our moral sense. We are far, far more than animals. But where does that morality come from?

Human beings are moral creatures because God created us in His image. That means we can choose between good and evil because God chooses between good and evil. We can think on a higher level, contemplating abstracts and ideals like goodness and nobility, because our minds are reflections of God's unimaginably complex mind. We can choose to love others by serving them sacrificially because that's what God is like, and He made us like Himself.

Why do people do bad things? Dr. Laura thinks it's because we're lapsing into our animal natures.[12] But we are not the product of evolution. We were never animals. We do bad things because we are born as fallen image-bearers. I love the way Larry Crabb described it: "When Adam sinned, he disfigured both himself and all his descendants so severely that we now function far beneath the level at which we were intended. We're something like an airplane with cracked wings rolling awkwardly down a highway rather than flying through the air. The image has been reduced to something grotesque. It has not been lost, just badly marred."[13]

But our airplanes continue to wander off the runway and go their own way because of the sinful nature that rules us. That's why we do bad things.

Although Dr. Laura is right about man being a moral creature, she misses the boat on what it means to be human when she says, "When Adam and Eve were in the Garden they were not fully human because they made no choices between right and wrong, no value judgments, no issues of ethics or morality. Leaving Eden, though, meant becoming fully human."[14]

They certainly did make a moral choice in the Garden. They chose wrong over right and chose disobedience over fellowship with God. Actually, when Adam and Eve were still living in the Garden, they were more fully human than we've ever been since, because God created man sinless, perfect, and beautiful. When we look at the Lord Jesus, the Second Adam, we see just how sinless, perfect, and beautiful "fully human" is.

Dr. Laura is right to insist that we see ourselves as moral creatures, because a moral God has made us in His image.

Dr. Laura's Wisdom

Dr. Laura's strong positions on certain topics has made some people stand up and applaud her while others fume in frustration at her bluntness.

She makes no bones about the sanctity of marriage and that sex belongs only within a committed relationship sealed with a sacred vow. People living together and having sex without marriage are "shacking up." She's right because God ordained sex to be contained in a safe relationship, and there are forty-four references to fornication (sex outside of marriage) in the Bible.

Another of her well-known positions is that abortion is wrong because it's killing a baby. The much better alternative is adoption. She gets particularly frustrated with women who say, "Oh, I could never do that. I could never give up my baby once it was born." Her answer to that is, "You can kill it but you can't wave good-bye?" Here again, she's right because abortion is the deliberate taking of a human life. God's Word clearly commands us not to murder (Exod. 20:13).

Her strong views on abortion continue in her commitment to children, and her disdain for the way so many parents pursue their own whims and agendas at the expense of their kids. In a day when divorce is so prevalent, she makes an impassioned case for doing what's best for the children, with parents remaining active and involved in the raising of their kids. She believes that the family is the cornerstone of civilization, and this is consistent with the biblical view, starting right in the first chapter of Genesis.

Part of the way parents should take care of their children is to make sure they raise them in a religious faith shared by both parents. Dr. Laura warns people not to enter into interfaith marriages because usually the kids end up with no religion at all. Both the Old and New Testaments warn against being unequally yoked; God knows it's a recipe for heartbreak at best and disaster at worst.

She shows practical wisdom in many ways. She makes a distinction between those who are evil and those who are merely weak. In the same way, the book of Proverbs goes into great detail about the difference between the wicked and the foolish.

Another evidence of her wisdom is her response to the fact that some people are uncomfortable keeping secrets, believing it's dishonest to not tell everything you know. Dr. Laura says there is a difference between maintaining privacy and withholding truth. The question to ask is, Will this benefit the person I tell? If not, don't tell. The reason this works is that this is how God operates. Everything He tells us in His word is truth, but it's not the whole truth. Plus, God doesn't owe it to us to tell us everything He knows, and He's not being dishonest when He keeps information from us, like the whys of our trials and sufferings, or the exact details of how the end times will play out.

Finally, Dr. Laura exhorts people to choose "as if" behavior. "What a radical idea: choosing how to behave regardless of how you feel—and discovering that behaving differently seems to change how you feel."[15] Second Corinthians 5:7 tells us to "live by faith, not by sight," which is another way of saying we should act as if something were already true instead of being limited by our feelings. I do love Dr. Laura's practical wisdom.

Where Dr. Laura Is Wrong

Most of the time, Dr. Laura's views are right on the mark because they are consistent with the laws and values of Scripture. She is still developing her own belief system, being a fairly recent convert to conservative Judaism, and she can be fair and open-minded in considering other viewpoints. But there are some areas where she departs from the Bible's teachings.

Dr. Laura believes that all religions are equally expedient for establishing morality. If a young mother calls, looking for a religion in which to raise her children, Dr. Laura doesn't care if it's Hinduism or Islam or Presbyterianism, just as long as there is a religion. To her the issue is what works, or what seems to work, and most religions are the same to her in the area of shaping behavior. On the other hand, the truthfulness of religious claims is apparently not as important to her. Yet only one religion offers a personal relationship with God on His terms, by His own definition. Only one religion is God reaching down to man: Christianity, with its roots in Judaism.

Dr. Laura is often wrong in her understanding of Christianity. She rejects the notion that Jews can believe in Christ. Many rabbis teach that to be Jewish is to reject Jesus as Messiah; they teach that Jesus is the God of the Gentiles. Two thousand years of unjust persecution feeds a heartbreaking "anti-Jesus" mentality. But Jesus Christ was a Jew, and almost all of the first believers were Jewish. As one messianic rabbi put it, to believe in the Jewish Messiah is the most Jewish thing someone can do![16] Dr. Laura is mistaken about this. When Jewish people trust Christ as Savior, they don't stop being Jewish. What they discover, in an intensely personal way, is that Judaism is the root, and Christianity is the fruit. They feel "completed" in ways many Gentiles never can.

What is the purpose of life? Dr. Laura has told many people who are floundering, because they lack personal meaning, that they need to find their niche in life to do their job, which is to perfect the world. This sounds noble, but there is nothing in Scripture that calls us to perfect an unperfectable world. In fact, God plans on scrapping the whole thing and starting over (Rev. 21:1). Perfecting the world is not our purpose in life. The reason we are here is to bring glory to God by fearing Him and keeping His commandments, as Ecclesiastes 12:13 tells us.

One other area where Dr. Laura misses the boat is in

dealing with guilt. I remember one caller who was filled with remorse and regret over her abortion. She asked Dr. Laura what to do with the guilt. Dr. Laura's belief system doesn't offer a way of handling it, and she advised the woman to just carry the guilt. This is her usual advice in such circumstances because she believes the person will learn a deep life lesson from the continual pain. I grieve that she has no understanding of the cleansing that comes with Christ's forgiveness. Jesus paid for our sins on the cross, and when we come to Him in belief and trust, He not only forgives the sin but cleanses us of the guilt. We don't have to carry guilt that He washed away!

Dr. Laura fills a need in society. Sometimes she departs from Scripture; Christians must then depart from her attitudes. But for the most part, Dr. Laura is usually right, and, as she likes to say, "Now, go take on the day!"

Part 3
Marriage and Family Issues

12

Men
Are from Mars,
Women
Are from Venus?

Ray and Sue Bohlin

Sue: Counselor John Gray made a ton of money—and attracted countless grateful fans—in writing his best-selling book *Men Are from Mars, Women Are from Venus.*[1] This book explored the intrinsic differences between men and women in a way that has helped millions of people understand why relationships between the two sexes can be so frustrating!

Ray: In this chapter we'll be examining some of the insights from this book, then looking at what the Bible says about how God wants men and women to relate to each other. It's no surprise that, since God created us to be different, He knew all about those differences thousands of years ago when He gave very specific instructions for each gender!

Sue: The whimsical premise of *Men Are from Mars* is that many years ago, all men lived on Mars, and all women lived on Venus. Once they got together, they respected and enjoyed their differences—until one day everybody woke up completely forgetting that they had once come from different planets. And ever since, men mistakenly expect women to think and communicate and react the way men do, and women expect men to think and communicate and react the way women do. These unrealistic expectations cause frustration. But when we understand the God-given differences between male and female, we have more realistic expectations of the other sex, and our frustration level drops.

Ray: Speaking of which, we do realize that it can be very frustrating for some people when gender differences are painted in such broad strokes, since there's such a broad spectrum of what women are like and what men are like. Both men and women come in different shapes and sizes, but by and large, we feel that most will identify with these characteristics.

Sue: With that said, let's look at some of the differences between men and women.

How Men and Women Differ

Ray: Men get a sense of self from achievement. We tend to be task oriented, and being self-reliant is very important to us. You put those two together, and you get people who hate to ask for directions or for help. I'll wander in a store for fifteen minutes trying to find something on my own, because accomplishing the task of getting a certain item isn't going to be satisfying unless I can do it myself. For us, asking for help is an admission of failure; we see it as a weakness.

Sue: Women get a sense of self from relationships. Where men are task oriented, we are relationally oriented. Our connections to other people are the most important thing to us. Instead of prizing self-reliance, we tend to be interdependent, enjoying the connectedness to other people, especially other women. For us, both asking for help and offering it is a compliment; we're saying, "Let me build a bridge between us. I value you, and it'll bind us together."

Ray: Men usually focus on a goal. We want to get to the bottom line, to the end of something.

Sue: But women tend to enjoy the process. Not that reaching a goal isn't important, but we like getting there too. That's why driving vacations are so very different for men and women; the guys want to get to their destinations and beat their best time with the fewest stops, and we sort of treasure the time to talk and look and maybe stop at the outlet malls along the way!

We believe these admittedly broad-brushed differences are rooted in God-created traits. In fact, some Christian authors like Gary Smalley and Stu Weber have addressed them in their books as well.[2]

Ray: Men are competitive. Big shock, huh? Whether we're on the basketball court or on the highway, we just naturally want to win, to be out front. Many of us are driven to prove ourselves, to prove that we're competent, and it comes out in a competitive spirit.

Sue: And it's not that girls aren't competitive, because of course we are; it's just that we tend to be more cooperative than competitive. When girls are playing and one gets hurt, the game will often stop and even be forgotten while everyone gathers around and comforts the one who went down. It's that relational part of us coming out.

Ray: Men are often more logical and analytical than women.

Sue: And we tend to be more intuitive than men. This isn't some sort of mystic claim; there was a study at Stanford University that discovered women catch subliminal messages faster and more accurately than men.[3] Voilà—intuition.

Ray: This difference is evident in brain activity. Men's brains tend to show activity in one hemisphere at a time . . .

Sue: . . . Where women's brains will show the two hemispheres communicating with each other, back and forth, constantly. That means that often, men and women can arrive at the exact same conclusion, using completely different means to get there. Our thinking has been accused of being convoluted, but it works!

Ray: Men are linear. We can usually focus on just one thing at a time. That's why Sue's learned not to try to talk to me while I'm reading the paper. It's a struggle for me to read and listen at the same time.

Sue: Yes, I've learned to get Ray's attention and ask if I can talk to him so it'll be an actual conversation and not a monologue! God made us women to be multitaskers, able to juggle many things at once. It's a requirement for mothering, I've discovered. Many times I'd be cooking dinner and helping the kids with homework and answering the phone and keeping an ear on the radio, all at the same time.

Ray: Men tend to be compartmentalized, like a chest of drawers: work in one drawer, relationships in another drawer, sports in a third drawer, and so on. All the various parts of our lives can be split off from each other.

Sue: Whereas women are more like a ball of yarn where everything's connected to everything else. That's why a woman can't get romantic when there's some unresolved anger or frustration with her husband, and he doesn't see what the two things have to do with each other.

Ray: One more thing: men are action oriented. When we feel hostile, our first instinct is to release it physically. And when we're upset, the way for us to feel better is to actively solve the problem.

Sue: Women are verbal. (Another big surprise, huh?) Our hostility is released with words rather than fists. And when we're upset, the way for us to feel better is by talking about our problem with other people.

Ray: When men are under stress, we generally distract ourselves with various activities. That's why you see so many men head for the nearest basketball hoop or bury themselves in the paper or TV. But there's another aspect of the way we handle severe stress that can be particularly frustrating to women who don't understand the way we are: a man withdraws into his "cave." We need to be apart from everybody else while we figure out our problems alone. Remember, a man is very self-reliant and competitive, and to ask for help is weakness, so he will first want to solve the problem by himself.

Sue: We women handle stress in the exact opposite way, which of course is going to pose major problems until we understand this difference! When we're stressed, we get more involved with other people. We want to talk about what's upsetting us, because we process information and feelings by putting them into words. But merely talking is only half of it; we talk in order to be heard and understood. Having a good listener on the other end is extremely important. No wonder there is such misunderstanding when people are under stress. As a friend of ours put it, "Men head for their cave, and women head for the back door!"

Ray: John Gray gave some great advice. He said that when a man's going into his cave, he can give powerful assurance to the woman in his life by telling her, "I'll be back."

Sue: Works for me! What's next?

Ray: A man's primary need is for respect. A man needs respect—trust, acceptance, appreciation, admiration, approval, and encouragement—both from his peers and from the significant women in his life. A man needs to know he's respected. He also needs to be needed. That's why it's so devastating to a man when he loses his job. He gets his sense of self from achievement, and he needs to be needed, so when the means to achieve and provide for his family is taken away, it's emotionally catastrophic.

Sue: It's good for us women to know that, so we can be grace-givers in a time of awful trauma. I think that just as a man is devastated by the loss of his job, a woman is devastated by the loss of a close relationship; both losses reflect the God-given differences between us. Just as a man needs to be respected, we primarily need to be cherished. Cherishing means giving tender care, understanding, respect, devotion, validation, and reassurance. We need to know others think we're special. And just as a man needs to be needed, we need to be protected. That's why security is so important to us. A man needs to be able to provide, and a woman needs to feel provided for.

Ray: One final difference. For men, words are simply for conveying facts and information.

Sue: But for women, words mean much more. They are not just to convey information, but to explore and discover our thoughts and feelings, to help us feel better when we're upset, and it's the only way we have to create intimacy. To a woman, words are like breathing!

Women's Needs and Issues

Ray: We have been examining how God created men and women to be different. So it's not surprising to find how much of our uniqueness and how many of our needs are addressed by God's commands and precepts in the Bible.

Sue: In this section we'll consider women's needs and issues, and look at how God's commands fit perfectly with the observations we've made. In the next section, we'll look at men's needs.

As I said, our primary need as women is to be cherished —to be shown TLC, understanding, respect, devotion, validation, and reassurance.

Ray: And in Ephesians 5:25, we read God's command that addresses this need: "Husbands, love your wives, just as Christ loved the church and gave himself up for her." When we think about the way Christ loves the church, we see a sacrificial love, a tender love, and a love that is committed to acting in the church's best interests at our Savior's own expense. God doesn't just want men to love their wives like they love sports—He wants us to love our wives in a way that makes them feel cherished and special. He wants us to love our wives with a sacrificial love that puts her needs and desires above our own.

First Peter 3:7 gives further instruction along this line: "You husbands likewise, live with your wives in an understanding way"(NASB). The Greek literally reads, "Dwell with them according to knowledge." The only way to live with your wife in an "understanding way" is to seek to know her. And when a husband listens and responds to what his wife shares—remembering that women are created to be verbal —she will feel cherished and understood and loved.

The last part of 1 Peter 3:7 continues, "Live with your wives in an understanding way, as with a weaker vessel, since she is a woman." This isn't a slam on women. When we read this verse, we ought to think along the lines of a fine china cup. It's definitely weaker than a tin cup, but that's because it's so fragile, delicate, and far more valuable. When we serve dinner on our china, we're very careful in handling it, and extremely protective of washing and drying it. We treat our china with tenderness and gentleness because of its fragility and value. That's how we cherish it. And that's how a man is to treat his wife—not roughly or carelessly, but with tenderness and gentleness, because God made women to be treated with special care.

Sue: The flip side of needing to be cherished is our need for security. We need to be protected and provided for. Even when a wife works, she wants to know that her husband is the main provider, or at least truly wants to be and is working to that end. The burden of being forced to provide for our families is bigger than we should have to bear.

Ray: God created that need for security within women. That's why He puts such a high value on the provisional aspect of a man's character. First Timothy 5:8 says, "If anyone does not provide for his relatives, and especially for his immediate family, he has denied the faith and is worse than an unbeliever." God wants men to be diligent workers and providers. He created us to bear the burden of providing; women are to be protected from that burden whenever possible.

Men's Needs and Issues

Ray: Men's primary needs are for respect and support— to receive trust, acceptance, appreciation, admiration, approval, and encouragement.

Sue: I think God intends for wives to meet those needs by submitting to their husbands, as they are commanded to do in Ephesians 5:22 and 1 Peter 3:1. Submission doesn't mean giving in or being an overworked doormat; it's a gift of our will. It means submitting to God first, then demonstrating that submission by choosing to serve and respect our husbands, always being their number one supporter. Even when a man is more of a jerk than a Superman, he needs the respect of his wife, even if she has to ask the Lord for His perspective on what areas of his life are worthy of respect!

It's interesting to me that in Ephesians 5, at the beginning of the passage on marriage, Paul exhorts women to submit to their husbands as to the Lord, and then closes this section by saying, "And the wife must respect her husband" (v. 33). Submission and respect aren't the same thing, but they're both necessary to meet a man's God-given needs. In the middle of this "marriage sandwich" is the awesome command for men to love their wives sacrificially and tenderly, as Christ loves the church. What I see is that offering submission and respect is a natural response to that kind of love.

Ray: Another aspect of men's constitution is that we're action oriented, whereas women are verbal.

Sue: Yes, and that's why I'm very intrigued by the wisdom of Peter's admonishment to women, where he says, "You wives, be submissive to your own husbands so that even if any of them are disobedient to the word, they may be won without a word by the behavior of their wives, as they observe your chaste and respectful behavior" (1 Peter 3:1-2 NASB).

To men, words are cheap—and if they're coming from a woman, all too plentiful! What impresses a man is what people do, not what they say. So here the Holy Spirit inspired Peter to basically tell us to shut up and live holy lives, which is the only language that's going to have a true impact on a man.

Ray: Another characteristic of men is that we tend to be self-oriented, as opposed to women who are more relational.

Sue: It's interesting to me that Paul exhorts men to love their wives as they love themselves and their own bodies (Eph. 5:28, 33). And he does this without condemning them for that self-orientation; he just uses it as a point of reference to demonstrate how powerfully men are to love their wives. From what I've observed at the health club about the way some men love their bodies, God wants men to indulge their wives with some major pampering!

Ray: One last comment. While men and women may be constitutionally different by design, we do share one important and serious flaw: our sin nature. Both genders are prideful and selfish. And that is one reason we find commands to both men and women to serve the other sex. But in the midst of our service, we can certainly enjoy the differences God gave us!

13

Why Marriages Fail

Kerby Anderson

Why do marriages fail? While the answers to that question are many, there is a growing body of empirical research suggesting there are four negative risk factors that create barriers to oneness in marriage and increase a couple's chances for marital failure.

I am going to look at these risk factors and see how they can be corrosive elements to oneness in marriage. Most of the material I will cover comes from PREP, which stands for the Prevention and Relationship Enhancement Program developed at the University of Denver. The material was originally published in a book entitled *Fighting for Your Marriage* and has been featured on numerous TV news magazine programs like "20/20." A Christian version of this material has been written by Scott Stanley; it is entitled *A Lasting Promise: A Christian Guide to Fighting for Your Marriage.* Perhaps you have heard professionals who speak on marriage, such as Gary Smalley and Dave and Claudia Arp, recommend this book.

The significance of this research is twofold. First, it provides reliable information on what makes marriages fail. Other Christian books, though very helpful, are often based upon the opinions and spiritual insights of the authors. The material we will be talking about in this chapter is based on clinical studies that validate biblical principles others have only discussed.

Second, the research provides an extremely accurate predictor of subsequent behavior and marital failure. In one of the key studies, researchers followed 135 couples for twelve years, starting before they were married. The researchers found that using data collected before the couples married, they were able to predict those couples who would do well and those who would not, with up to 91 percent accuracy. In other words, the seeds of distress and possible divorce were already sown before the couples went to the altar.

Now please do not be discouraged by these numbers. At the outset it seems to be telling us that certain marriages are doomed to failure, and there is nothing a couple can do. But we need to reconsider that conclusion. This research, while showing us marriages which might fall apart, does not suggest that there is nothing we can do about it. It simply shows us what behaviors can be changed and warns us what will probably happen if we are unwilling or unable to change. As the book of James reminds us, it is not enough to just believe something, we must act upon it (James 1:25; 2:15–17; 3:13).

Since knowing precedes acting, it is necessary to discuss these four negative risk factors that can be barriers to oneness, for oneness is God's design for marriage. Genesis 2:24 says, "For this reason a man will leave his father and mother and be united to his wife, and they will become one flesh." When Jesus was confronted by the scribes and Pharisees about the issue of divorce, He brought them back to this foundational truth and said, "For this reason a man will leave his father and mother and be united to his wife, and the two will become one flesh. So they are no longer two, but one. Therefore what God has joined together, let man not separate" (Matt. 19:5-6).

Negative Behavior Patterns

According to the research carried out over the last two decades, negative patterns can destroy a relationship. Couples who want to save their marriage need to focus on changing these negative behavior patterns. There are four such patterns I will discuss here, the first of which is escalation.

Escalation

According to the researchers, "escalation occurs when partners respond back and forth negatively to each other, continually upping the ante so the conversation gets more and more hostile."[1] First Peter 3:9 says, "Do not repay evil with evil or insult with insult." But this is exactly what happens with escalation. Each negative comment increases the level of anger and frustration, and soon a small disagreement blows up into a major fight.

Research shows that couples who have a good marriage are less prone to escalation. And if the argument starts to escalate, they are able to stop the negative process before it erupts into a full-blown fight. On the other hand, some couples find that arguments escalate so that damaging things are said that may even threaten the lifeblood of the marriage.

Escalation can develop in two different ways. The first is a major shouting fight that can erupt over a conflict as small as putting the cap back on the toothpaste. As the battle heats up, the partners get more and more angry, saying mean things about each other. Frequently there are threats to end the relationship. Over time, those angry words damage oneness, and angry threats to leave begin to seem like prophecy. Once negative comments are made, they are hard to take back and can drive a knife into the partner's heart. Proverbs 12:18 says, "Reckless words pierce like a sword."

Reckless words can do great damage to a marriage because when an argument escalates, every past event and vulnerable point becomes fair game. Concerns, failings, and old mistakes are now be used by the attacking partner. Oneness and intimacy can be shattered quickly by a few reckless words.

You may say, "We don't fight like cats and dogs." And while that may be true, your marriage may still have this risk factor. Damaging escalation is not always dramatic. Voices do not have to be raised for couples to get into a cycle of returning negative for negative. Paying the rent, taking out the garbage, running errands, any conflict that results in muttering to yourself, rolling your eyes, or throwing up your hands can also be examples of escalation.

Couples who escalate arguments must control their emotions and control their tongues. James writes, "If anyone considers himself religious and yet does not keep a tight rein on his tongue, he deceives himself and his religion is worthless" (1:26). Couples who want a strong marriage must learn to counteract the tendency to escalate as a couple. The key to a strong and stable marriage is learning to control your emotions and your tongue.

Invalidation

The second of the four negative risk factors to oneness is called invalidation. "Invalidation is a pattern in which one partner subtly or directly puts down the thoughts, feelings, or character of the other."[2]

Invalidation can take many forms. Sometimes it can be caustic, in which one or both partners attack the other person verbally. You can hear, and even feel, the contempt one partner has for another.

Sarcastic phrases like "Well, I'm sorry I'm not perfect like you" or "I forgot how lucky I am to be married to you" can cut like a knife. These are attacks on the person's character and personality that easily destroy a marriage. Research has found that invalidation is one of the best predictors of future problems and divorce.

Jesus taught that our attacks on a person's character are sinful and harmful. "But I tell you that anyone who is angry with his brother will be subject to judgment. Again, anyone who says to his brother, 'Raca,' is answerable to the Sanhedrin. But anyone who says, 'You fool!' will be in danger of the fire of hell" (Matt. 5:22). Calling a person worthless or empty-headed (which is what the Aramaic term *raca* means) is not what a Christian should do.

Invalidation can also be much more subtle. It may involve an argument where contempt for the other partner is not so obvious. One partner may merely be putting the other partner's feelings down. The message conveyed is that your feelings do not matter. A husband may put his wife down because she is more emotional or because she is more easily hurt by comments. He may invalidate his wife's fears about the children's safety. A wife may invalidate a husband's desire to succeed in the company, saying that it really doesn't matter if he becomes district manager. Ultimately the partner receiving these comments begins to share less and less so that the level of intimate sharing evaporates. When this happens, oneness is lost.

Sometimes invalidation may be nothing more than trite clichés like "It's not so bad" or "Just trust in the Lord." While the sayings may be true, they invalidate the pain or concern of the other partner. They make the other partner feel like their fears or frustrations are inappropriate. This kind of person is what Solomon called "one who sings songs to a heavy heart" (Prov. 25:20). When one partner is hurting, the other partner should find words of encouragement that do not invalidate his or her pain or concerns.

The antidote to invalidation is validation. Couples must work at validating and accepting the feelings of their spouse. That does not mean you have to agree with your spouse on the issue at hand, but it does mean that you listen to and respect the other person's perspective. Providing care, concern, and comfort will build intimacy. Invalidating fears will build barriers in a marriage. Discipline yourself to encourage your spouse without invalidating his or her feelings.

Negative Interpretations

The third risk factor is negative interpretations. "Negative interpretations occur when one partner consistently believes that the motives of the other are more negative than is really the case."[3]

Such behavior can be a destructive pattern in a relationship and can quickly erode intimacy and oneness in a marriage. A wife may believe that her husband does not like her parents. As a result, she may attack him anytime he is not overly enthusiastic about visiting them. In reality he may only be concerned with the financial cost of going home for Christmas or about whether he has enough vacation time. She, in turn, thinks his behavior displays a dislike of her parents.

When a relationship becomes more distressed, the negative interpretations mount and contribute to an environment of hopelessness. The attacked partner gives up trying to make himself or herself clear and becomes demoralized.

Another kind of negative interpretation is mind reading. "Mind reading occurs when you assume you know what

your partner is thinking or why he or she did something."
Nearly everyone is guilty of mind reading at some time or
other. When you mind read positively, it does not do much
harm. But when you mind read on the negative side, it
can spell trouble for a marriage.

Paul warned against attempting to judge the thoughts
and motives of others (1 Cor. 4:5). And Jesus asked, "Why
do you look at the speck of sawdust in your brother's eye and
pay no attention to the plank in your own eye?" (Luke 6:41).

Negative interpretations are hard to detect and counteract. Research shows that in distressed marriages, partners
tend to discount the positive things they see, attributing
them to causes such as chance rather than to positive characteristics of the partner. That is why negative interpretations do not change easily.

The key to battling negative interpretations is to reconsider what you think about your partner's motives.
Perhaps your partner is more positive than you think. This
is not to advocate some unrealistic "positive thinking"
program, but rather to encourage a realistic assessment of
negative assumptions you may be bringing to the marriage.

Did your spouse forget to do what you asked? Was it
intentional or accidental? Does he or she try to annoy you
or are you being more critical than is warranted? Most of
the time, people think they are doing the best they can. It
hurts to be accused of doing something hurtful you never
intended. For couples to have a good marriage, this pattern
of negative interpretation must be eliminated.

Often this is easier said than done. First, you have to
ask yourself if your thinking might be overly negative.
Do you give your spouse the benefit of the doubt? Second,
push yourself to look for evidence that is contrary to your
negative interpretation. Often it is easier to see his or her
speck than your own plank. Give your mate the benefit of

the doubt rather than let inaccurate interpretations sabotage your marriage.

Withdrawal and Avoidance

The last risk factors identified by researchers at the University of Denver are withdrawal and avoidance. These are two different manifestations of the problem wherein a partner is unwilling to get in or stay in a discussion that is too threatening.

"Withdrawal can be as obvious as getting up and leaving the room or as subtle as 'turning off' or 'shutting down' during an argument. The withdrawer often tends to get quiet during an argument, look away, or agree quickly to a partner's suggestion just to end the conversation, with no real intention of following through."[4]

"Avoidance reflects the same reluctance to get into certain discussions, with more emphasis on an attempt not to let the conversation happen in the first place. A person prone to avoidance would prefer that the topic not come up and, if it does, may manifest the signs of withdrawal just described."[5]

In a typical marriage, one partner is the pursuer and the other is the withdrawer. Studies show that it is usually the man who wants to avoid these discussions and is more likely to be in the withdrawing role. Sometimes the roles reverse. But, for the sake of this discussion, we will assume that the husband is the one who withdraws.

Why does he withdraw? Because he does not feel emotionally safe to stay in the argument. Sometimes he may even be afraid that if he stays in the discussion or argument he might turn violent, so he retreats.

When the husband withdraws, the wife feels shut out and believes that he does not care about the marriage. In other words, lack of talking equals lack of caring. But that is often a negative interpretation about the withdrawer.

He, on the other hand, may believe that his wife gets upset too much of the time, nagging and picking fights. This is also a negative interpretation because she, as pursuer, really wants to stay connected and resolve the issue he does not want to talk about.

Couples who want to have a good marriage must learn to stay engaged. Paul said, writing to the church in Ephesus, "Therefore each of you must put off falsehood and speak truthfully to his neighbor, for we are all members of one body. In your anger do not sin: Do not let the sun go down while you are still angry, and do not give the devil a foothold" (Eph. 4:25–27).

Although the immediate context in this passage is anger, the principle can be applied here. It is important not to let avoidance become a corrosive pattern in your marriage. Couples should build oneness and intimacy by speaking openly and honestly about important issues.

Conclusion

Each of these four risk factors—escalation, invalidation, negative interpretations, and withdrawal and avoidance—can build barriers in a marriage, leading ultimately to loneliness and isolation. The research shows that couples who want a good marriage need to eliminate these risk factors, or else the negative factors will overwhelm the positive. It is never too late to put your marriage back on track.

For further study on this topic, I recommend that you obtain Scott Stanley's book *A Lasting Promise: A Christian Guide to Fighting for Your Marriage* (San Francisco: Jossey-Bass, 1998). This book is a good source for help in establishing and maintaining the oneness that God desires for every marriage.

14

Marital Reminders

Jerry Solomon

N umerous books, essays, magazine articles, radio and television commentaries, and sermons have been dedicated to the subject of Christian marriage. In light of the tragic divorce rate and the continuing struggles that are experienced by many couples, this is not surprising. Marriage is a subject that has immediate application to a large portion of the population. The comments that are offered in this chapter are not necessarily intended to provide new perspectives. They are intended to serve as reminders to all of us, no matter what our marriage may be like. After all, few of us can stay "on track" at all times. We sometimes need a gentle or not-so-gentle nudge to return to what God intends for His creation: good, strong marriages.

Foundational Truths About Marriage

The first reminder focuses on what we will call "foundational truths." These truths are found in two passages in the first two chapters of Genesis.

The first passage is Genesis 1:26–28. It states that both the man and the woman were created in God's image. This affirms the dignity of both sexes. Human beings are the zenith of creation; men and women are uniquely blessed by God.

The second passage is Genesis 2:18–25. It asserts several truths that are applicable to the marriage union. First, the woman was fashioned from the fiber of the man, and she was created as an equal but also as a helper for him. Upon observing the newly created woman, the man reacted in a way that indicates he recognized her very special significance. We can only imagine his joy and excitement when he first caught a glimpse of her. Second, God affirms the marital union by commanding that couples are to leave their parents. The priorities are changed; a new family is to be formed. Third, the couple is to cleave together and become one flesh, an affirmation of the sexual union in marriage. But it is to be much more than simply a sexual union; it is to be a holistic union, a union of the total person, both material and immaterial, a "oneness."

These two passages from Genesis should spur us to better appreciate how highly God values marriage and how we should as well. The fact that we are made in God's image means we should reverence and respect each other. If it is true that my spouse is made in God's image, that should prompt me to treat her with great respect and honor. She is not an accidental being; she is specially related to the Creator of the universe. When I treat her with reverence, I am paying homage to God.

Also, God's foundational instructions should lead us to live with a sense of commitment to our spouses that transcends any other earthly relationship. If we are to leave our parents, if we are to cleave to our spouses, and if we are to be one flesh, then we must remember that such concepts are unique. Thus I am giving myself to the most important person in my life. I don't think of returning to my parents physically or emotionally; I don't cleave to anyone else the way I cleave to my wife; I am not one flesh with anyone other than her. And the beauty of all this is that God has given us these commands for our own good. They constitute the first steps to marital fulfillment.

Biblical Symbiosis

Another marriage reminder centers on what we call "biblical symbiosis." Symbiosis is "two different organisms living in close association or union, especially where such an arrangement is advantageous to both." An illustration of symbiosis from the animal kingdom may be helpful here. There is, for example, a particular species of fish that spends its life in close proximity to the mouth of a shark. In fact, it eats from the shark's teeth. (This keeps the shark from making too many visits to the dentist.) On the other hand, most of us have had to deal with the irritating result of a mosquito's attack. The mosquito is an example of parasitism, "a relationship in which one organism lives off another and derives sustenance and protection from it without making compensation."

Which of these two illustrations should serve as an example of Christian marriage? Surely most of us would reply that symbiosis, not parasitism, should be the correct model. Unfortunately, this model is not always lived out in spouses. The results of a parasitic relationship are devastating. Many can testify to this.

The Bible, of course, provides insights that remind us of how the proper model for marriage should be constructed. First, Galatians 3:28 asserts that there is "neither male nor female," and all are "one in Christ Jesus." And 1 Peter 3:7 states that husbands should treat their wives as "heirs with you of the gracious gift of life." Thus Christian couples should remember that they are spiritual equals with sexual differences.

Second, we should follow Christ's model. The Lord put Himself in subjection to His earthly parents (Luke 2:51–52) as well as to His heavenly Father. He adapted Himself to earthly orders. Even though He was total deity, He humbled Himself for our benefit (Phil. 2:1–11). In addition, 1 Corinthians 11:3 indicates that Christ modeled the concept of "necessary headship" in that God is the head of Christ.

Third, we need to be reminded that all things are subjected to Christ (Eph. 1:22–23). This includes His body, the church, of which the Christian couple is a part. Thus a proper view of authority and subjection begins with our allegiance to Christ, the head of the church.

Several thoughts come to mind with regard to these biblical perspectives, and all of them revolve around the attitude and character of Christ Himself.

Wouldn't it be odd to think that Christ viewed us based upon whether we were male or female? He didn't die for males before females, or vice versa. In our relationship to Him there is no sexual distinction. The Christian couple should take this to heart; there is not to be a "lording over" each other; there is to be no spiritual pride.

It is clear that both spouses are to remember that subjection is the responsibility of all Christians. The Lord has demonstrated this perfectly. The couple begins with this foundation; then they discover how to combine subjection with a proper view of authority within the family, a concept we will discuss next.

According to our definition of symbiosis, then, Christian marriage should be composed of two different people in a loving union that is based upon subjection first to Christ and then to one another. Surely such an arrangement will prove to be advantageous to both.

Responsibilities

What's a wife to do? What's a husband to do? Does

the Bible provide specific guidelines for each? The answer is a resounding, Yes! Our continuing review of "marriage reminders" brings us to the third of them, which we will simply call "responsibilities."

The wife's responsibility is most succinctly stated in Ephesians 5:22–24. The term "subjection" is the summary word for her. She is to submit to her husband. It is important to note that the verb for subjection is found in verse 21; then it is implied in verse 22. And verse 21 states that all Christians are to "be subject to one another in the fear of Christ" (NASB). As we stressed earlier, subjection applies to all of us. But verse 22 does stress that the wife is to have a particular attitude toward her husband.

Another very important element of this verse is not stressed often enough. We cannot honestly approach this verse without emphasizing the latter part of it: "as to the Lord." The wife's subjection is first of all to the Lord, then to her husband, because this is the Lord's pragmatic plan for marriage. She is to respect the headship of her husband because this is God's idea, not her husband's. This is not demeaning. It is godly. Her self-esteem is not based upon her husband; it is based upon her place in the sight of God. An important analogy exists here. She is to recognize that her husband is said to be her head "as Christ is the head of the church" (v. 23). The wife should recognize this analogy and realize that her husband has been compared to the compassionate and perfect Christ. He has a grave responsibility, and she needs to encourage him by following God's design for her.

Compared to the wife's responsibility, the husband has a sobering and challenging one. His role is also outlined in Ephesians 5:25–33. The most important aspect of this role can be found in the Greek term agape, "love," which is used to describe how a husband is to respond to his wife. It is important to note that the word is used in the imperative mood. Thus, it is a strong command which involves action, not just feeling. This love must be demonstrated, just as God demonstrated His love by giving His son (John 3:16). Also, a humbling analogy is given. The husband is to "agape" his wife as Christ "loved the church and gave Himself up for her." This entails action and sacrifice. The husband is to show his wife that he loves her because she is worth sacrificing himself for. What an awesome responsibility—a responsibility that should be humbling for those husbands who would use their authority as head of the home to treat their wives in a tyrannical manner. This does not imply that the husband's authority is weakened. Husbands are still in a position of headship, but that headship should mean they are to treat their wives as "heirs with you of the gracious gift of life." As with the wife's role, the husband's role demonstrates God's pragmatic plan for marital life.

So the responsibilities are clear: the wife is to submit "as to the Lord"; the husband is to love as Christ loved.

Communication

Most married couples are in need of another very important reminder. Their relationship requires communication. The joy of marriage stems from a commitment that is communicated. This vital principle can be related in many ways. We will share three of them.

First, the couple must learn to talk with one another. Perhaps that sounds simple, but don't let its simplicity fool you. Actually, too many couples experience a deteriorating relationship because they have lost their ability to relate verbally. In my many years in the ministry, it has become obvious to me that one of the major flaws in Christian marriages is a lack of conversation involving anything beyond the absolute necessities. Too many couples don't really know each other. Often they are total strangers.

Each spouse has a need to express the deepest longings of the heart and soul with his or her lifetime companion. Sometimes this requires a great deal of effort and courage, especially for a partner who is not accustomed to being vulnerable. But the effort offers wonderful results. Sharing thoughts, ideas, complaints, doubts, fears, expectations, plans, dreams, joys, and even frustrations can lead to a deepening bond that, in turn, leads to a stronger marriage.

This type of communication requires concentration. It should take place without interference. Each spouse should give undivided attention to the other. If one is talking, the other must listen. That's the only way communication can be successful.

Second, couples need to be reminded to communicate better sexually. God has given us the joy of expressing marital commitment by "becoming one flesh." This rich phrase is certainly meant to refer to sex in marriage, but we cannot forget that the type of sex that we are designed to experience involves more than just a physical act. It also involves the most intimate form of human communication. The Song of Songs, for example, is full of expressions that indicate the beauty of communication including, but also transcending, the physical. Proverbs 5:15–19 contains many expressions of intimacy, such as forms of the words "rejoice," "satisfy," and "captivate," all of which emphasize both the physical and nonphysical aspects of sexual intimacy. A spouse must "control his own body in a way that is holy and honorable" (1 Thess. 4:4). These words entail something beyond the physical. It would be difficult, for example, for a man to honor his wife sexually without communicating love, appreciation, patience, compassion, and many other attitudes that are much needed by her.

Third, most marriages can benefit from communication that is unspoken and nonsexual. Meaningful glances, unexpected flowers, cards sent for no reason other than as an expression of love, a gentle touch; these are the ways of communicating that can sometimes mean the most. They are stored in a couple's memory bank, to be withdrawn and enjoyed again and again.

It is helpful to note that nonverbal communication often leads to or reinforces verbal and sexual communication. A certain glance can be very romantic; an unexpected flower can recapture a special day; a card can spur significant verbal communication.

The couple that learns to communicate verbally, sexually, and by gestures will experience the joy of marriage.

Little Things Mean a Lot

"Little things mean a lot" is a maxim with a lot of meaning for marriage. Most husbands and wives can benefit from remembering this. The following lists include some of those "little things." Consider which of them could be helpful in your marriage. Wives, in particular, are often deeply touched and encouraged by such things. And husbands respond positively when their wives take the time to do the little things that mean so much.

Little Things for Wives to Do

- Pray for your husband daily.
- Show him you love him unconditionally.
- Tell him you think he's the greatest.
- Show him you believe in him.
- Don't talk negatively to him or about him.
- Tell him daily that you love him.
- Give him adoring looks.
- Show him that you enjoy being with him.

- Listen to him when he talks with you.
- Hug him often.
- Kiss him tenderly and romantically at times.
- Show him that you enjoy the thought of sex.
- Show him you enjoy meeting his sexual needs.
- Take the sexual initiative at times.
- Express interest in his interests.
- Fix his favorite meal at an unexpected time.
- Demonstrate your dedication to him in public.
- Do things for him he doesn't expect.
- Show others you are proud to be his wife.
- Rub his back, legs, and feet.
- Stress his strengths, not his weaknesses.
- Don't try to mold him into someone else.
- Revel in his joys; share his disappointments.
- Show him your favorite times are with him.
- Show him you respect him more than anyone.
- Don't give him reason to doubt your love.
- Leave "I love you" notes in unexpected places.
- Give him your undivided attention often.
- Tell him he is your "greatest claim to fame."
- Let him hear you thank God for him.

Little Things for Husbands to Do
- Say "I love you" several times a day.
- Tell her often she is beautiful.
- Kiss her several times a day.
- Hug her several times a day.
- Put your arm around her often.
- Hold her hand while walking.
- Come up behind her and hug her.
- Always sit by her when possible.
- Rub her feet occasionally.
- Give her a massage occasionally.

- Always open doors for her.
- Always help her with chairs, and so on.
- Ask her opinion when making decisions.
- Show interest in what she does.
- Take her flowers unexpectedly.
- Plan a surprise night out.
- Ask if there are things you can do for her.
- Communicate with her sexually.
- Show affection in public places.
- Serve her breakfast in bed.
- Train yourself to think of her first.
- Show her you are proud to be her husband.
- Train yourself to be romantic.
- Write a love note on the bathroom mirror.
- Call during the day to say "I love you."
- Always call and tell her if you will be late.
- Let her catch you staring lovingly at her.
- Praise her in front of others.
- Tell her she is your "greatest claim to fame."
- Let her hear you thank God for her.

Of course these lists are not exhaustive. The number of things that can be done to build up a marriage is limitless. When our imaginations are active, we can discover exciting and uplifting ways to experience the wonder of marriage.

Marriage needs to be built on God's foundational truths. These truths tell us that marriage should be a relationship that blesses each partner, that specific responsibilities are given to the wife and husband, that communication is one of the important building blocks of a strong marriage, and that little things mean a lot.

May God bless us as we strive to put these reminders into practice.

15

When Your Teen Rejects Your Values

Rick Rood

Mark Twain once advised parents that when their children turn thirteen, the parents should put them in a barrel, close the lid, and feed them through a hole in the side. When they turn sixteen, Twain suggested, parents should close the hole! Twain was a humorist, and we laugh about his counsel. But beneath the laughter is the recognition that the teenage years are seldom easy—for teens or their parents! And it's particularly challenging when parents find that their teen is rejecting their values.

Admittedly, in tackling this issue we are taking on a real lion! If there is anything more humbling than being the parent of a rebelling teenager, it's attempting to pass on advice to others who are struggling with this same situation. But our prayer is that this chapter will offer some help and encouragement to parents of a challenging teen.

"Adolescence" is the label we attach to the time of life from the onset of puberty to maturity. It denotes the stage of life during which a young person moves from childhood to adulthood, from dependence upon parents to independence. It's a time of great change physically, emotionally, mentally, spiritually, and socially. It's a time when teens are asking questions like "Who am I?" "What do I believe?" "How do I fit into life in this world?" while they're searching for their identity as individuals.

Adolescence is also a time when some degree of strain develops between teens and their parents. No longer do parents appear to be infallible and beyond contradiction. Our flaws are much more visible, and probably exaggerated, to our teen. It's a time when the values of their peers generally appear much more attractive than do those of their parents, and when acceptance by their friends will likely become much more important than acceptance by their parents.

It is not uncommon, in their quest for identity and independence, for teens to reject some of the values of their parents, their church, and society. And to a degree this is not unhealthy. Young people need to develop their own convictions about life. And part of the process may involve challenging the values and convictions they have been taught. Some may challenge them more overtly, and others more covertly. Some may challenge them in relatively minor areas such as dress, appearance, music, or the way they keep their room. Others may show total disregard for the moral and spiritual values of their family, their church, and even society.

Parents who allow for no individuality in some of the "minor" areas (such as dress and appearance), may be challenging their teen to test them in areas that are of much greater consequence.

Several years back, a group that included Dr. James Dobson conducted a survey of some thirty-five thousand parents. The survey concluded that while 25 percent of teens were of "average" temperament, 40 percent were considered to be more "compliant," and 35 percent were more "strong-willed." (More boys than girls fell in this latter category.) Among the strong-willed teens, 74 percent were found to be in some degree of rebellion during their teenage years, 26 percent of them to a severe degree. Furthermore, it was found that the strong-willed were most susceptible to the influence of their peers! It was no surprise to find that 72 percent of parents of strong-willed teens characterized their relationship as "difficult" or "very stressful."[1]

If you identify with this group of parents, you are definitely not alone. And perhaps this realization is an important first step in responding to a teen who rejects our values.

The Sources of Teenage Rebellion

Many parents have wondered if the teen living in their home is really the same child that they played with and enjoyed just a few years before. And it is only natural for them to ask why: "Why is this happening? And why is this happening to us?" Most parents are probably also asking themselves, "Where did we go wrong? What could we have done to prevent this from happening?" These questions are not only painful to ask, but are equally difficult to answer. And it's important not to jump to simplistic conclusions in trying to do so.

It is very likely that there is more than one reason why our teen is rejecting our values. And there really are many possible reasons. One that we noted is that it is simply the nature of adolescents to search for their own identity and independence. We also noted the role that innate temperament plays in teenage rebellion. There are, however, a number of other possible reasons why a teen is rejecting our values. It's important to look beyond their behavior to the reasons behind it.

Physiological Factors

First, it's possible that there are physiological factors involved. Young people who have learning disabilities or attention deficit/hyperactive disorder (AD/HD) are going to be much more inclined to rebel, in part over the frustration they are experiencing in meeting the expectations of their parents, teachers, and other authority figures. Any physical illness, or even an imbalanced or insufficient diet, can affect a teen's emotional and behavioral patterns. Even apart from such irregularities, the changes that are taking place in an adolescent's hormonal system are apt to result in more volatile emotions.

Psychological Factors

Second, it is possible that there are difficulties of a psychological nature, or even disorders of a more serious nature involved. In this latter category would fall young people who are manic-depressive or schizophrenic. It is important to realize that many of these disorders have genetic and biological sources, requiring the attention of a medical professional. It is more likely, however, that a teen may be struggling with low self-esteem or depression, and may be engaging in conduct that is aimed at obtaining the acceptance of his peers or gaining the attention of his parents or other authority figures (even if it's negative in nature).

Outside Tensions

Third, it is not uncommon for a young person to express his anger (and even guilt) over the tensions that may exist within the family at large, or between his parents, by acting in a rebellious fashion.

Traumatic experiences such as a death in the family, prolonged illness, or serious financial problems can be a source of rebellion. They may even result in a teen's questioning the existence or the goodness of God, and in rejecting God's moral principles.

We must not fail to mention the negative influence of peers and of the values portrayed and endorsed in today's movies, television, and the lyrics of much of the music that young people listen to. All of these media are communicating a message that, more often than not, challenges the right of anyone (including parents) to limit their freedom or stifle their individuality.

Parenting Styles

Finally, it is not impossible that our own example as parents or our parenting style has contributed to their rebellion to a greater or lesser degree. It is not uncommon for Christian parents to feel that we bear the greater (if not exclusive) share of responsibility when teens reject our values. After all, haven't we been taught that if we "train a child in the way he should go, . . . when he is old he will not turn from it" (Prov. 22:6)? If they do turn from the way they should go, certainly it is our fault for not training them properly!

At the outset, we must affirm that parents are responsible before God for providing the training and instruction that will guide children in His way. The Scriptures also warn us not to "exasperate your children" (Eph. 6:4) or to "embitter your children, or they will become discouraged" (Col. 3:21). When our teen is rebelling, it's appropriate for us to evaluate the impact that our own parenting style has had in our child's life.

We must just as emphatically, however, reject the notion that teenage rebellion is invariably the consequence of parental mismanagement. To believe that it is, is to accept the premise that all human behavior is caused by external influences. Behavior may be influenced (even strongly) by genetic and environmental factors, but to say that there is no such thing as human will and choice is to deny a fundamental element of biblical teaching. In the final analysis, a young person's rejection of godly values is a personal choice.

Many Christians, however, find themselves adopting an essentially behavioristic and deterministic philosophy in their interpretation of the "train up a child" proverb. Many parents have concluded from this proverb that if their teen does turn from the way he should go, it is because they have failed to provide the training he needed. But that this proverb should be taken as a general observation about life (as should many proverbs), rather than as an absolute divine promise, can be deduced from two facts.

First, if we do take this proverb as an absolute promise, then other proverbs in the book must be taken this way also. Yet there are a number of proverbs for which exceptions can be found on a regular basis. For example, Proverbs 10:27 says, "The fear of the LORD adds length to life, but the years of the wicked are cut short." This is a general truth. But there are innumerable examples of the wicked who have lived long on the earth, and of the godly whose lives have been cut short.

Second, to take the proverb as an absolute promise would contradict the teaching of many other proverbs that it is possible for a young person to reject the training his parents provide. Proverbs 15:5 says, "A fool spurns his father's discipline." The writer of Proverbs also appeals to sons to "accept" and "store up" their parents' instruction (2:1–2), and warns not to "forsake" their parents' teaching (4:1–2; see also Deut. 21:18–21).

We must conclude, then, that when our teens reject our values, we must prayerfully discern to what degree both we and they are responsible for what is happening, as well as what other influences are at work. In some cases, the parents may bear a great deal of responsibility; in others they may bear very little. The important thing, however, is not so much who is to blame, but what should be done from this point on in our relationship with our teen.

A Plan for Parents

Get Help

Our first response to a challenging teen must be to look beyond the rebellious behavior to the sources that lie behind it. If we suspect there are factors of a physiological nature, we must not neglect to enlist the help of a qualified physician. Nor should we reject the aid of a godly counselor in addressing issues of depression or self-image that may lie hidden in our teen's heart. But neither should we neglect to look to the Scriptures as our ultimate source of wisdom.

Start with You

As we do, it will be tempting to look initially for ways in which we can promote change in our teenager's behavior. But the one factor in our child's life over which we have the most influence is our own character and approach to parenting. And this is where we must begin—by reflecting on the model which God Himself provides in His character and in His relationship with us as His children. In God our Father we find that perfect balance of judgment and grace, discipline and love, compassion and firmness. This is the standard against which all of us fall short, the one we will never fully attain in this life; but it also is the one by which we must measure our lives, and toward which we must continually strive! Larry Crabb has said, "The key to becoming a more effective parent is to become an increasingly godly person."[2] Wise are the parents who makes this their primary goal!

Apologize

Wise, too, are the parents who resist the impulse to project a perfect image, but who echo the prayer of David: "Search me, O God, and know my heart. . . . See if there is any offensive way in me, and lead me in the way everlasting" (Ps. 139:23–24). Wise are the parents willing to offer a sincere apology and to seek forgiveness for genuine short-comings. But wise also are the parents who refuse to brood over failures, and who, having learned from mistakes, set out in a new direction (Phil. 3:13–14). And wise, too, are the parents who guard against trying to atone for past mistakes by becoming overly permissive.

Show Unconditional Love

As we seek to allow God to shape our lives after His own model as the divine parent, we will do well to keep two primary qualities in view. The first is an unconditional love for our child. This is the kind of love God manifests toward us. "But God demonstrates his own love for us in this: While we were still sinners [while we were his enemies], Christ died for us" (Rom. 5:8). This is the kind of love He seeks to instill in us for our teenagers, regardless of how much anger or contempt they have shown toward us—a love that asks not how they can meet our requirements, but how God can use us to minister to their genuine needs.

Discipline in Love

The second quality is an uncompromising commitment to help our teenager grow toward responsible maturity. "The Lord disciplines those he loves; . . . but God disciplines us for our good, that we may share in his holiness" (Heb. 12:6, 10). As God guides us in the path of righteousness and establishes clear expectations for our lives, so must we do for our teen. As God disciplines those who rebel through appropriate consequences, so also must we.

But how do unconditional love for our teens and an uncompromising commitment to guide them toward responsible maturity take shape in our day-to-day lives? How do we show this kind of love toward our teenager?

First, we love them when we praise and reward them for the good that we do see in their lives, as God does with us. We love them when we show respect for their feelings and opinions, though not always agreeing with them. We love them when we show interest in and participate in activities that are meaningful to them, and refrain from squeezing them into a mold for which they were not designed. We love them when we keep our anger from erupting into violent acts and hurtful words, when we relate as a "fellow struggler," when we don't try to be better than they are at everything, when we handle our own sin in the same way we expect them to handle theirs, when we listen to their explanations before disciplining them, when we keep alive a sense of hope and excitement about discovering God's purpose for their lives!

But the love toward which we strive is also one that guides and disciplines (Prov. 13:24): "He who loves [his son] is careful to discipline him." Researchers have found that teens are less likely to rebel when they grow up in homes that are neither too permissive nor overly authoritarian, where parents gradually allow participation in decisions as they gradually relinquish responsibility, all the while maintaining final authority.[3]

What are a few marks of parents who have this kind of

commitment? First, they provide instruction in the ways of the Lord. One teenager who refused to accompany his family to church was willing to read a chapter of Scripture with his father several times a week. By his senior year, they had read through the entire New Testament together!

Second, they communicate clear expectations regarding personal conduct (even if the parents of their child's friends do not): expectations concerning the use of language in the home; honesty about activities; household chores; attendance at school; curfew; use of the car; payment for gas; insurance and traffic tickets; drinking; and sexual conduct.

Finally, such parents will enforce meaningful consequences for willful rebellion. There are some things we are obliged to provide for our child no matter what: a place to live (though it need not be our own home in all situations), food, clothing, and personal respect. But many things that young people take for granted today are privileges that can and must be suspended in the event of irresponsible behavior: use of the phone or TV, tuition for school, use of your car, or even the privilege of holding a driver's license. Teenagers who engage in activities that are not only irresponsible but illegal, should have every expectation that their parents will notify the authorities. We do our children no favor when we shield them from the painful consequences of foolish choices. Some teens become skilled at manipulating their parents through guilt or intimidation. But we must resolve to render such tactics ineffective by refusing to let them work.

God does not hold us responsible for all of our teenagers' actions. He holds us accountable for the way in which we relate to them as parents—with unconditional love, but with an uncompromising commitment to responsible maturity.

Yet, even when we do all this, God provides no guarantee that our teens will always (or even ever) respond positively. But He does ask that we persist in doing what is right: praying for them, gradually relinquishing them to Him—He knows them far better than we—remembering His exhortation that we "not become weary in doing good, for at the proper time we will reap a harvest if we do not give up" (Gal. 6:9).

Resources

Campbell, Ross. *How to Really Love Your Teenager.* Wheaton: Victor, 1983.

Dobson, James. *Parenting Isn't for Cowards.* Waco: Word, 1987.

Greenfield, Guy. *The Wounded Parent.* Grand Rapids: Baker, 1991.

Huggins, Kevin. *Parenting Adolescents.* Colorado Springs: NavPress, 1992.

Kageler, Len. *Teen-Shaping: Solving the Discipline Dilemma.* Old Tappan, N.J.: Revell, 1990.

Kesler, Jay, ed. *Parents & Teenagers.* Wheaton: Victor, 1984.

White, John. *Parents in Pain.* Downers Grove, Ill.: InterVarsity, 1979.

Endnotes

Chapter 1

1. Warren Leary, *The New York Times,* 9 February 1989.
2. "American Teens Speak: Sex, Myth, TV, and Birth Control," *The Planned Parenthood Poll,* Lou Harris and Associates, September-October 1986, 13.
3. David Van Biema, "What You Don't Know About Teen Sex," *People,* 13 April 1987, 110-21.
4. Barbara Dafoe Whitehead, "The Failure of Sex Education," *Atlantic Monthly,* October 1994, 55-80.
5. Ibid., 57.
6. Ibid., 69.
7. Lawrence Criner, "Safer Sex Ads Downplay Risks," *Insight,* 9 May 1994, 22.
8. Ibid.
9. Ibid.
10. Ibid.
11. Tom McNichol, "Sex Can Wait," *USA Weekend,* 25-27 March 1994, 4-6.
12. Centers for Disease Control, 1992, *Morbidity and Mortality Weekly Report,* 8 April 1994, 231-33.
13. Dinah Richard, *Has Sex Education Failed Our Teenagers?* (Pasadena, Calif.: Focus on the Family, 1990), 59-60.
14. Larry Withan, "As Washington Pushes Safe Sex, Others Preach Abstinence," *Washington Times,* 3 October 1993, A4.

Chapter 2

1. Medical Institute for Sexual Health, Austin, Texas.
2. I. W. Stout et al., *Pediatrics* 83 (1989): 376-79.
3. Joe S. McIlhaney Jr., *Safe Sex* (Grand Rapids: Baker, 1991), 86.

Chapter 4

1. Erich Fromm, *The Art of Loving* (New York: Harper & Row, 1956).

2. Robert R. Bell, *Premarital Sex in a Changing Society* (Englewood Cliffs, N.J.: Prentice Hall, 1966), 150.

3. Eric L. Dey, Alexander W. Astin, and William S. Korn, *The American Freshman: Twenty-Five Year Trends, 1966-1990* (Los Angeles: Higher Education Research Institute, 1991), 21.

4. Gallup Youth Survey, "The Religious Beliefs and Sexual Attitudes and Behavior of College Students," The Gallup Organization, 1989.

5. Evelyn Duvall, *Why Wait Till Marriage?* (New York: Association Press, 1965), 38.

6. William H. Masters et al., *The Pleasure Bond* (New York: Bantam, 1976), 113-14.

7. Howard Hendricks, lecture, Dallas Theological Seminary, 1978.

8. Michael McManus, "Churches: Wedding Factories or Marriage Savers?" *National and International Religion Report,* 1 November 1993, 1.

Chapter 6

1. Joe Dallas, *A Strong Delusion: Confronting the "Gay Christian" Movement* (Eugene, Ore.: Harvest House, 1996).

2. Dr. Judith Reisman, "Kinsey and the Homosexual Revolution," *The Journal of Human Sexuality* (Carrollton, Tex.: Lewis and Stanley, 1996), 21.

3. Ibid., 26.

4. Ibid., 21.

5. Richard G. Howe, *Homosexuality in America: Exposing the Myth,* American Family Association site, www. For 1-3 percent rate see J. Gordon Muir, "Homosexuals and the 10% Fallacy," *Wall Street Journal,* 31 March 1993; Tom W. Smith, "Adult Sexual Behavior in 1989: Number of Partners, Frequency of Intercourse and Risk of AIDS," *Family Planning Perspectives,* The Alan Guttmacher Institute, May-June 1991, 102; John O. G. Billy, Koray Tanfer, William R. Grady, and Daniel H. Klepinger, "The Sexual Behavior of Men in the United States," *Family Planning Perspectives,* The Alan Guttmacher Institute, 25, no. 2 (March-April 1993).

6. Jeffrey Satinover, "The Gay Gene?" *The Journal of Human Sexuality.*

7. Dallas, *Strong Delusion,* 114.

8. Ibid., 112-14.

9. Ibid., 116.

10. Ephesians 5:25-32.

11. John 20:30.

12. Dallas, *Strong Delusion,* 193.

13. Ibid., 195.

14. Peter LaBarbera, "The Gay Youth Suicide Myth," *The Journal of Human Sexuality.*
15. Ibid.
16. Ibid., 66.
17. Ibid., 67.
18. Ibid., 68.

Chapter 7

1. Diane Medved, *The Case Against Divorce* (New York: Donald I. Fine, 1989), 1-2.
2. National Center for Health Statistics, "Advance Report of Final Divorce Statistics, 1983," *NCHS Monthly Vital Statistics Report* 34, no. 9 (26 December 1985): table 1.
3. Landon Jones, *Great Expectations: America and the Baby Boom Generation* (New York: Ballantine, 1980), 215.
4. Ibid., 216.
5. Cheryl Russell, *100 Predictions for the Baby Boom* (New York: Plenum, 1987), 107.
6. Judith Wallerstein and Sandra Blakeslee, *Second Chances: Men, Women and Children a Decade After Divorce* (New York: Ticknor and Fields, 1989).
7. Sheila Fitzgerald Klein and Andrea Beller, *American Demographics,* March 1989, 13.
8. William Dunn, "I Do, Is Repeat Refrain for Half of Newlyweds," *USA Today,* 15 February 1991, A-1.
9. "Families: Neo-Nukes," *Research Alert,* 17 August 1990, 6.
10. "When the Family Will Have a New Definition," What the Next 50 Years Will Bring, a special edition of *United States News and World Report,* 9 May 1983, A-3.
11. Arland Thornton and Deborah Freedman, "The Changing American Family," *Population Bulletin* 38, no. 4 (Washington, D.C.: Population Reference Bureau, 1983), 10.
12. Lynn K. White and Alan Booth, "The Quality and Stability of Remarriages: The Role of Stepchildren," *American Sociological Review* 50, no. 5 (October 1985): 689-98.
13. G. J. Wenham, "Gospel Definitions of Adultery and Women's Rights," *Expository Times* 95, no. 11 (1984): 330.

Chapter 8

1. Sherry Hite, *Women and Love: A Cultural Revolution in Progress* (New York: Alfred Knopf, 1987), 365, 412.

2. Frank Pittman, *Private Lies: Infidelity and the Betrayal of Intimacy* (New York: Norton, 1989), 117.

3. Ibid., 13.

4. Kenneth Woodward, "Sex, Morality and the Protestant Minister," *Newsweek,* 28 July 1997, 62.

5. "How Common Is Pastoral Indiscretion?" *Leadership,* winter 1988, 12.

6. In this poll Americans were asked: What is your opinion about a married person having sexual relations with someone other than his or her spouse? Their answers: 79 percent answered "always wrong" and another 11 percent answered "almost always wrong." "Attitudes on Adultery," USA Today/CNN/Gallup Poll, 1997.

7. Willard Harley, *His Needs, Her Needs: Building an Affair-Proof Marriage* (Grand Rapids: Revell, 1994).

8. Pittman, *Private Lies,* 122.

9. Bonnie Eaker Weil, *Adultery: The Forgivable Sin* (Norwalk, Conn.: Hastings House, 1994), 9.

10. Pittman, *Private Lies,* 37.

11. Ibid., 53.

Chapter 9

1. Christina Hoff Sommers, *Who Stole Feminism?* (New York: Touchstone, 1994).

2. Gloria Steinem, *Revolution from Within* (Boston: Little, Brown, 1992), 222.

3. Naomi Wolf, *The Beauty Myth* (New York: Doubleday, 1992), 180-82.

4. Joan Brumberg, *Fasting Girls: The Emergence of Anorexia Nervosa as a Modern Disease* (Cambridge, Mass: Harvard University Press, 1988), 19-20.

5. Women's Studies Network (Internet: listserv@umdd.umd.edu), 4 November 1992.

6. *Time,* 18 January 1993.

7. *Boston Globe,* 29 January 1993, 16.

8. Catherine MacKinnon, "Sexuality, Pornography, and Method," *Ethics,* January 1989, 331.

9. Camille Paglia, "The Return of Carry Nation," *Playboy,* October 1992, 36.

10. Peter Hellman, "Crying Rape: The Politics of Date Rape on Campus," *New York,* 8 March 1993, 32-37.

11. *The New York Times,* 9 January 1991, B6.

12. "A Call to Action: Shortchanging America" (Washington: American Association of University Women, 1991).

13. *The AAUW Report: How Schools Shortchange Girls* (Washington: AAUW Educational Foundation, 1992).

14. *Boston Globe,* 2 February 1992.

Chapter 10

1. Toni Grant, *Being a Woman: Fulfilling Your Femininity and Finding Love* (New York: Random House, 1988).

2. Ibid., 3.

3. Physicians of the Geisinger Health System, "Motherhood at Thirty Something." http://www.geisinger.edu/ghs/pubtips/MotherhoodatThirtySomething.html

4. Denise Mann, "Older Women Rarely Become New Moms with IVF." http://www.ssnewslink.com/demo/womensstudies/19980226A3555.html

5. Andreas Kostenberger, "Saved Through Childbearing?" *The Council on Biblical Manhood and Womanhood News,* September 1997, 3.

6. John Gray, *Men Are from Mars, Women Are from Venus* (New York: HarperCollins, 1992).

7. Grant, *Being a Woman,* 9.

8. Mary Kassian, *The Feminist Gospel* (Wheaton, Ill.: Crossway, 1992), 159.

Chapter 11

1. Laura Schlessinger, *How Could You Do That?* (New York: HarperCollins, 1996), 8.

2. Ibid., 134.

3. Ibid., 269.

4. "No Whining!" *United States News and World Report,* 14 July 1997.

5. Schlessinger, *How Could You Do That?* 152.

6. Laura Schlessinger, *Ten Stupid Things Women Do to Mess up Their Lives* (New York: HarperCollins, 1995), 171.

7. Ibid., 157.

8. Ibid., 189.

9. Don Matzat, *Christ Esteem* (Eugene, Ore.: Harvest House, 1990), 173.

10. C. S. Lewis, *Miracles* (New York: Macmillan, 1960), 52.

11. Schlessinger, *How Could You Do That?* 26.

12. Ibid., 187.

13. Larry Crabb, *Understanding People* (Grand Rapids: Zondervan, 1987), 87.

14. Schlessinger, *How Could You Do That?* 93

15. Ibid., 257.

16. Personal conversation with the staff of *Baruch Ha Shem,* a messianic congregation in Dallas, Texas.

Chapter 12

1. John Gray, *Men Are from Mars, Women Are from Venus* (New York: HarperCollins, 1992).

2. Gary Smalley, *Hidden Keys to a Loving, Lasting Marriage* (Grand Rapids: Zondervan, 1984); and Stu Weber, *Tender Warrior* (Sisters, Ore.: Multnomah, 1993).

3. Smalley, *Hidden Keys,* 17.

Chapter 13

1. Scott Stanley et al., *A Lasting Promise: A Christian Guide to Fighting for Your Marriage* (San Francisco: Josey-Bass, 1998), 29.

2. Ibid., 32.

3. Ibid., 35-36.

4. Ibid., 40.

5. Ibid., 40-41.

Chapter 15

1. James Dobson, *Parenting Isn't for Cowards* (Waco, Tex.: Word, 1987), chaps. 3-4.

2. Kevin Huggins, *Parenting Adolescents* (Colorado Springs, Colo.: NavPress, 1992), 258.

3. Len Kageler, *Teen Shaping* (Old Tappan, N.J.: Revell, 1990), chaps. 3, 12.

Other great books in this series include . . .

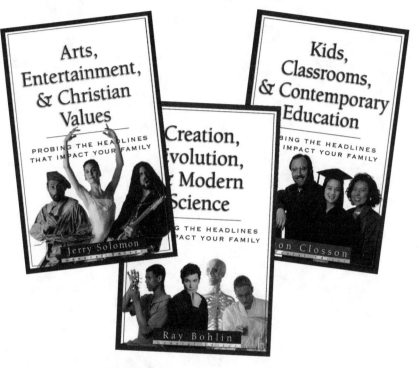

Arts, Entertainment, and Christian Values
Jerry Solomon, general editor
ISBN 0-8254-2032-6

Creation, Evolution, and Modern Science
Ray Bohlin, general editor
ISBN 0-8254-2033-4

Kids, Classrooms, and Contemporary Education
Don Closson, general editor
ISBN 0-8254-2034-2

Available at your local Christian bookstore or at

kregel
PUBLICATIONS

PO Box 2607, Grand Rapids, Michigan 49501